Lives cut short

Lives cut short
Child death by maltreatment

Marie Connolly
and
Mike Doolan

© Marie Connolly and Mike Doolan

Published in 2007 by
Dunmore Publishing Ltd
PO Box 25080
Wellington
books@dunmore.co.nz
for the Office of the Children's Commissioner
Wellington.

National Library of New Zealand Cataloguing-in-Publication Data

Connolly, Marie.
Lives cut short : child death by maltreatment / Marie Connolly
and Mike Doolan.
Includes bibliographical references and index.
ISBN 978-0-909039-22-3
1. Children—New Zealand—Death—Case studies.
2. Child abuse—New Zealand—Case studies.
3. Abused children—Services for—New Zealand.
I. Doolan, M. P. (Michael Patrick), 1943- II. Title.
362.7620993—dc 22

Text: Georgia 10/13
Cover design: Central Media, Wellington
Typesetting: Joanna Morton

Table of Contents

Acknowledgements

Projects of this kind invariably benefit from the support of a range of people and this book has been no exception. Conversations have occurred as we gathered research data, professionals have shared their knowledge with us, and colleagues have shared important insights. We thank all of the people who have contributed to our work in this way.

We would also like to thank some people specifically. We are most grateful to Richard Woollons, whose advice regarding the statistics was invaluable; to the Reverend Maurice Grey for his advice on cultural issues; and to Terrie Moffitt and Geoffrey Chambers who provided advice on their area of research. It goes without saying that any errors that may be found in the manuscript are entirely our own.

In addition we are grateful to staff from the Ministry of Social Development who shared their professional expertise with us, in particular Kelly Anderson, Jo Field, Nova Salomen and Megan Chapman from the Office of the Chief Social Worker. Our thanks also go to Child, Youth and Family for providing research access to the case study material, and to the New Zealand Police for their assistance with respect to police data.

Finally, we are grateful to Elizabeth Rathgen and George Hook, whose keen editorial skills have been evident in the production of the final manuscript. We appreciate the demands that this has placed upon already busy working lives.

The opinions expressed in this book are the professional opinions of the authors and do not necessarily reflect the official views of the Ministry of Social Development.

Marie Connolly and Mike Doolan

Preface

The life of each child that is cut short by the trauma of abuse or neglect is an indictment on our society. As His Honour Mick Brown wrote in his report in 2002, 'It represents the link between adult behaviour and children's pain'. It proves that their parents and families have failed to provide the fundamental duty of care to these children, and their pain signals our collective failure as a society to protect and nurture them. We need to improve our understanding of what is happening so that we are better able to protect these children and young people.

This book is the first comprehensive effort to understand child homicide in New Zealand by undertaking both a quantitative and qualitative analysis of child deaths by maltreatment. It allows us to paint a picture of the nature of the abuse, and make some comments about the responses. While it does not explain all of the links between individual patterns of behaviour and the wider contextual factors that affect families, such as socioeconomic status, cultural or gender behaviours and expectations, it places us on a good footing to further develop our knowledge of this most complex issue. It provides encouragement for us to think deeply about risk to children and to seek solutions that will help us to protect our most vulnerable members of society.

Mike Doolan has been the Chief Social Worker for the former Department of Social Welfare, and Dr Marie Connolly is the current Chief Social Worker within the Ministry of Social Development. Their practice and academic experience of statutory child protection places them in a unique position to understand what happens to abused children and young people and what needs to be done to address their needs.

My role as Children's Commissioner for New Zealand focuses on the promotion of the United Nations Convention on the Rights of the Child. As statutory advocate for children, I focus on the need to move beyond the basic rights that children have to survival, safety, health and education, to actively promoting the participation of children and developing a culture of respect for them. If children and young people are to grow up as healthy, well-adjusted and contributing future members of society, we must redouble our efforts to keep them safe. For some the battle for survival remains a major challenge. We need to speak up for these children, against those who ignore, hurt or humiliate them, and do our very best as parents, relatives and as a society to protect and nurture them.

Dr Cindy Kiro
Children's Commissioner
September 2007

Foreword

The family has been described as the foundation stone of society. It has also been described as a haven in a heartless world. When a child dies at the hand of a family member, especially a parent, our foundation stone is shaken and the notion of a haven becomes fragile. The impact goes far beyond those who knew and grieve for the child. Such deaths happen to a very small number of children in a society, and that it is not a new phenomenon matters little. The fact that there is no child protection system that can prevent all child abuse deaths, just as there is no mental health system that can prevent all suicides, similarly matters little. Because each child is precious we are compelled to ask collectively 'how might this tragedy have been prevented?'

Marie Connolly and Mike Doolan use New Zealand police data on 91 child homicides from 1991 to 2000 to explore this question. Given what is known from other countries about deaths resulting from child neglect, it is quite possible that the total number of child maltreatment deaths in New Zealand in this period was significantly greater than this. The malnourished baby suffering from failure to thrive who develops pneumonia and dies from lack of medical attention does not appear in homicide statistics. Nor are fatal acts of omission recorded in this way.

Connolly and Doolan bring to the task a balance and wisdom much needed in the field of child protection. Using a systems framework they examine a broad range of factors that influence the safety of a child, from the family to the service system. The data give a partial and complex picture, leaving many questions unanswered.

Why is there such a marked over-representation of Māori children in these fatalities? Why do young boys seem to be at much greater risk of fatal injury from their mother's male partner when he is not the biological father? How significant is post-natal mental illness in cases of infanticide by mothers? What is the role of alcohol in triggering domestic violence and child assault? What part is played by win–lose custody disputes in child homicide–parental suicide cases?

There are many questions that need to be answered. The fundamental one, of course, is what can we do? The answer is 'a lot'. We will not be able to prevent all child maltreatment deaths, but we can reduce the number. Just as fatalities and injuries from road trauma were dramatically reduced through painstaking analysis of data on accidents – from driver behavioural factors through to car and road design factors, so the successful prevention of child abuse and neglect will require rigorous research. Child homicide data and child protection death inquiries have taken us so far – a comprehensive child mortality review process, underpinned by strong population-based data will take us much further.

Improving medical responses to road trauma has saved lives but population-based strategies such as changing social norms in relation to drinking and driving, and improving car safety and road design have saved far more. This might be a useful metaphor for a public health approach to child abuse and neglect. While we need to enhance the response of child protection systems to those children who are identified as being very vulnerable, we are likely to find that the greatest gains will come from broader strategies.

These might include: reducing problem drinking through pricing policies, advertising restrictions and changing social norms in relation to alcohol and parenting; enhancing the capacity of universal maternal and child health services and general practitioners to reach all new mothers and identify post-natal mental illness; and working proactively with vulnerable men involved in custody disputes. Ultimately it is by strengthening kith and kin networks to perform their traditional role of protecting and nurturing children rather than by relying on surveillance by the state that we will protect most children.

This is a big agenda. It may take a decade or more. It will take political will and it will take community support. But it can be done and it must be done – in memory of the children who have died and for those not yet born.

Professor Dorothy Scott
Director of the Australian Centre for Child Protection
University of South Australia

Chapter 1

Introduction: Thinking about child homicide

The killing of children is a highly emotive subject. Children are among the most vulnerable in our society. Most rely entirely on adults to protect them. And, of course, most adults feel intensely protective. Writing about children who die through homicide[1] requires us to step back, as much as it is possible to do so, and explore the experiences of these children and the ways in which we respond to these tragic events. This is what we try to do in this book.

Over the past decade there has been mounting concern at the level of child abuse and, more particularly, at the number of children whose lives have been tragically cut short by homicide. The death of a child in violent circumstances gives rise to many questions – how prevalent is child homicide? What are the circumstances surrounding these tragic situations? How do services respond to the children and families involved? These are not unreasonable questions. Yet in New Zealand we have struggled to answer them, largely because of a lack of information and research that would deepen our understandings and knowledge of child homicide and our systems of response. Prior to the 1990s, the only available national collection of information about child homicide was in data recorded by the New Zealand Police. This changed in 1994 when the child welfare system began to systematically collect information about children who had some involvement with the services and who subsequently died from any cause. Previously, the central agency was only notified about high-profile deaths that raised media interest, or when children in the direct custody of the state died. Other deaths were responded to by social work staff in local centres who worked with the families helping them to cope with the dreadful loss. While this was of great importance, nevertheless it meant that a significant source of data about what happened to these children and their families was not examined in any routine way.

From 1994 onward, however, this information was collected centrally. It was found that children who died, and who had been involved in some way with statutory child protection services had, understandably, died from a range of causes. Children died from illnesses, and from accidents as well as from suicide and homicide. Indeed, some children were in the care of statutory services because they were seriously or terminally ill and this was the best way of ensuring their care until they died. Reviewing the deaths of children led to a better understanding of the circumstances surrounding their deaths, and enabled the community to be confident that child welfare services had done what they could to support and provide for the child and their family. Where services were found to be wanting in some way, it was hoped that learning from these tragedies would result in an improvement and a strengthening of child welfare practice and services for children in the future. While laudable in aim, it could also be argued that the very process of review contributed to a set of unintended and unexpected consequences.

Reviews became a source of official information that exposed the phenomenon of child homicide to the New Zealand community. Throughout the 1990s the news media provided the community with stories of children who had died in the most horrifyingly violent circumstances, and this built to a crescendo of alarm about child abuse in the latter half of the decade. Publicity around these deaths was often associated with an examination and criticism of statutory child welfare agency practices and perceived failings. While health, education and police professionals faced criticism, the most sustained and critical scrutiny focused on statutory child-welfare professionals. Where the agency itself had intended case reviews to provide an opportunity to improve practice, the media saw the reviews as the means of linking child death to instances of professional error or incompetence. In what Ferguson (2004) refers to as 'scandal politics', media pressure called for accountability from the staff concerned and the agency that employed them. We believe that this has been critical in the emergence of more risk-averse practices by child-welfare professionals, which may, paradoxically, increase the level of risk for highly vulnerable children, an argument we explore more fully in Chapter 4.

Increasingly, it seemed, the statutory agency charged with caring for our society's most vulnerable children became the agency not only associated with, but also arguably held responsible for, child deaths by the community. So great was public concern it is perhaps not surprising that people questioned whether, in fact, New Zealand was such 'a great place to raise children'. But it was becoming clear that the development of a blame culture in child protection was not just a New Zealand phenomenon. Many Western countries were experiencing similar problems as child welfare and protection systems under pressure found themselves overwhelmed with increased notifications of at-risk children (Connolly, 2004). It seemed that societal demands were increasingly expecting statutory systems to take responsibility for everything relating to the care and protection of children – an unsustainable expectation from an organisational perspective and of questionable benefit in terms of the real needs of vulnerable children and their families.

This sustained pressure does not create an environment within which a statutory agency can think reflectively about what is happening and why. Rather it induces a reaction that is in part defensive and in part reactionary, contributing to less effective and at times overly invasive services for children perceived to be at risk. Public, political and media pressures also often fail to acknowledge or recognise that the statutory system of child protection involves many agencies across a continuum of services for children and families.

This book has been written to help us think our way through the complex issues that surround and contribute to child homicide and to explore the ways in which we can respond to them.

In the first part of the book we focus on research that examines the prevalence and nature of child homicide. Chapter 2 reviews the international literature relating to children who die from maltreatment. Then in Chapter 3 we turn our attention to New Zealand, where a total of 91 children were killed during the decade between 1991 and 2000. Police statistical data relating to these deaths are examined in order to identify the characteristics of the children who died and the people who killed them. This analysis reinforces, in particular, the vulnerability of pre-school children, as over 60% of the children who died were younger than five years of age. Māori children were killed at a higher rate than non-Māori children, so we focus on trying to understand the reasons for this.

In the second part of the book we explore how services respond when a child dies from homicide. Even within the most diligent practice intervention, things can go wrong. And when they do go wrong, public reaction toward the professionals involved can be punitive. Under these circumstances it is perhaps not surprising if workers become less inclined to manage risk – less inclined to trust families and their ability to protect their own children. We consider these issues in Chapter 4, and, in particular, the impact that public scrutiny of child homicide events can have on the development of more risk-averse practices. Here we confront a major challenge: that our system may actually be harming some children even as it tries to protect them.

Continuing to look at the ways in which responses to child homicide evolve, the following two chapters consider child homicide in the context of New Zealand's statutory child welfare system. Chapter 5 looks at how statutory services seek to secure the safety of children in New Zealand. Managing risk in child protection and securing safety for children are complex endeavours, and it is not possible to make systems infallible. Decisions often reflect difficult judgements made under uncertain conditions with less than perfect options. This is the nature of social work within the statutory child protection setting. Social workers know only too well the damage that can be caused by unnecessarily removing children from their parents. Decision-making becomes a question of weighing this potential damage against what might happen to the child if left with his or her parents. This represents the daily complexity of child protection work and provides some sense of the dilemmas social workers experience regularly when considering the care and safety needs of children, which lays the foundation for understanding the case studies examined in the following chapter.

In Chapter 6 we report on a qualitative study of the nine deaths that occurred between 1996 and 2000 to children who were known to Child, Youth and Family (CYF), the agency with statutory responsibility for children at risk in New Zealand. The case studies reveal that all too often acts of violence towards children are difficult to anticipate. Furthermore, despite the relentless search for professional error when a child dies, we found that interventions failed for a variety of reasons – many of which were intrinsically associated with the family circumstances rather than the actions of professionals.

In Chapter 7 we look at what we can learn from the histories and experiences of child victims of homicide. Not surprisingly, what we find from the analysis of this information has implications for families and the agencies that support them. In this final chapter, we draw together what we consider to be the key issues arising from the research. We use these issues to look at where we might go from here in order to strengthen systems of response for children at risk so that all that is possible can be done to prevent further tragedies.

In the decade under study in the research that informs this book, 91 children had their lives cut short by violence. They were lost as sons and daughters, brothers and sisters, nieces, nephews, grandchildren, friends and neighbours. Inevitably their deaths have left a mark on the lives of the people close to them – whether they are family, friends or the professionals who have tried to support them. Sadly, but realistically, we will never be able to protect every child from all harm, but we can work towards ensuring that our systems are the best they can be in supporting families and protecting children. Perhaps then we will have a better chance of reducing the number of lives cut short.

Notes

[1] We define child homicide as the unlawful killing of a child aged 0 to 14 years. It is variously described as infanticide, death from maltreatment, manslaughter and murder.

Chapter 2

Patterns of child homicide

When a child meets a violent death in New Zealand one of the first questions asked is: are New Zealanders more violent to children than adults in other countries? It is a question that is never satisfactorily answered. Experts become equivocal when pressed by media wanting a straightforward answer. The problem is that statistics about child death by homicide present difficulties both with respect to interpretation and comparison. In this chapter we will discuss some of the difficulties inherent in making comparisons across international boundaries, and we will look at what we know about child homicide from an international perspective. As we will see, comparative analysis is by no means straightforward.

Child homicide classification and reporting issues

The international literature reveals a history of misdiagnosis of child homicide. What counts as homicide varies between different countries – for example whether a child death resulting from neglect qualifies as homicide – and there are recognised issues with under-reporting (Brookman & Nolan, 2006; Herman-Giddens, 2001; Krug, Dahlberg, Mercy, Zwi & Lozano, 2002; Schlosser, Pierpont & Poertner, 1992; Strang, 1996; Wilczynski, 1997). Of all the types of child homicide, infanticide – the killing of a child under one year of age by its mother or father – is the most susceptible to misclassification as a death by some other cause (Brookman & Nolan, 2006). Studies estimate, for example, that as many as 5–10% of children recorded as having died from Sudden Infant Death Syndrome may have been misdiagnosed incidents of parental neglect or abuse (Bass, Kravath & Glass cited in Pecora, Whittaker & Maluccio, 1992; Emery & Taylor cited in Brookman & Nolan, 2006). Further, as many as 20–30% of children who died in house fires may have died as a result of neglectful supervision (Brookman & Nolan, 2006; Mitchel cited in Pecora et al., 1992). Recent studies reported in the US estimate that as many as 50–60% of deaths that resulted from child abuse or neglect were not recorded as such, with neglect being the most unrecorded cause of maltreatment fatalities (Crume, DiGuiseppi, Byers & Sirotnak, 2002; Herman-Giddens, Brown, Verbiest, Carlson, Hooten et al. cited in National Clearinghouse on Child Abuse and Neglect Information [NCCAN], 2004). Death from neglect is more likely to be under-reported than death from abuse (Pecora et al., 1992). This may also be so in New Zealand. Only two of the 91 recorded homicide cases that occurred in the decade from 1991–2000 in this country identified neglect as the cause of death, and yet in the United States, where a concerted effort has been made to identify and report child deaths that result from caregiver neglect, almost two out of every five deaths regarded as homicide are attributed to neglect alone (NCCAN, 2004). It is possible that these US figures include deaths from what might be described as neglectful supervision – the drowning of infants in home swimming pools, for example – the sorts of incidents that in New Zealand are most likely to be classified as tragic accidents rather than culpable homicide.

Evidence suggests that under-reporting is only one aspect of the problem of determining the rate of child homicide incidents. Writers have also noted class and race bias influence which cases are reported as child abuse, raising further implications for the proper identification of child homicide by abuse (Newberger & Bourne, 1985). This is supported by one New Zealand study (Kotch, Chalmers, Fanslow, Marshall & Langley, 1993), which found an association between the ethnic-minority status of the victim and the labelling of the injury as child abuse.

A range of factors cause problems in attempting to rate countries relative to one another on the basis of their record of child maltreatment deaths. Under-identification, together with under-reporting and different standards of sensitivity to child abuse from country to country, and variations in the rigour of investigations more generally, have been noted (UNICEF, 2003). In probably the most comprehensive attempt at international analysis of child homicide patterns, UNICEF states:

> Inconsistencies of classification and a lack of common definitions and research methodologies mean that little internationally comparable data exist and that the extent of child maltreatment is almost certainly under-represented by the statistics. (UNICEF, 2003, p. 2)

There are also issues that affect the reliability and accuracy of child mortality data more generally. These include the varying reporting requirements within or between different administrations; differing definitions of neglect and abuse; variations in review or coronial processes; the amount of time (up to a year in some cases) to determine a link between the fatality and abuse or neglect; and the miscoding of death certificates (NCCAN, 2004).

Incidence of child homicide

Notwithstanding these problems, attempts have been made to better understand the global size and shape of lethal violence against children. In a major international study by Krug et al. (2002), it was estimated that there are 57,000 homicides of children under the age of 15 annually. This study also found that rates of fatal abuse vary according to the income level of a country and region of the world. Reported rates in low- to middle-income countries were found to be two to three times higher than rates reported in high-income countries, and rates were highest in the African region and lowest in the European, Eastern Mediterranean, and Western Pacific regions (Krug et al., 2002).

In an often-quoted analysis of child maltreatment deaths in rich or developed nations, UNICEF (2003, p. 2) found that '3,500 children less than 15 years of age die from maltreatment (physical abuse and neglect) every year in the industrialized world'. This study calculated child maltreatment mortality rates in OECD countries in four age bands: under 1 year; from 1–4 years; from 5–9 years; and from 10–14 years. These rates were then weighted with a common set of weights reflecting a standard OECD population. This resulted in an estimation of a mean child maltreatment death rate in New Zealand of 1.2 per 100,000 per annum for children between 0 and 14 years over the period 1994–1998. In descending order, from the lowest rate of child homicide to the highest, New Zealand was placed 25th out of 27 countries. Only the US and Mexico featured higher child homicide rates. When figures were revised to include child deaths 'of undetermined intent',[2] New Zealand's child maltreatment death rate rose to 1.3 per 100,000 children between 0 and 14 years but its position improved to 22nd out of 27.

Both positions, however, represent a deterioration in child homicide rates for New Zealand compared with the period 1971–1975 when the basis for the rankings was established. At that time our child maltreatment mortality rate was calculated at 0.9 per 100,000-child population, and New Zealand was in 9th position on a league table of 23 OECD countries. Between the two periods, New Zealand's rate deteriorated in comparison with Belgium, Sweden, Switzerland, Canada, Austria, Australia, the United Kingdom, Finland, Poland and Japan, and improved only in relation to Portugal.

While on the surface this seems to place New Zealand in a poor position in terms of child homicide rates, these international comparisons need to be interpreted with caution. Child death by homicide is a rare event, and in a small country such as New Zealand the very small numbers involved produce highly volatile rates. For example, in the five years from 1999 to 2003 the rate of child homicide declined back to 0.9 per 100,000 children on the basis of only three fewer child deaths per million children per year. A further decline to 0.8 per 100,000 children has been reported for the five years from

2000 to 2004 (MSD, 2007). Small changes in the absolute number substantially alter the rate of child deaths. This suggests that it is less than helpful, indeed it can sometimes be misleading, to use international comparisons.

Because the number of child homicides is very small relative to national populations, this makes it difficult to draw valid conclusions about the characteristics of children who are at risk of being killed through maltreatment. The fact that child homicide is so rare also means that trying to identify actual at-risk children in advance presents almost insuperable difficulties (UNICEF, 2003).

Child homicide as a proportion of all homicides

Little mention of the incidence of child homicide as a proportion of all homicides appears in the international literature. This is an important issue as it raises the question of whether violence against children is linked to the overall incidence of violence in a particular society.

An international study of violence revealed that of the estimated 520,000 homicides that occurred globally during 2000, 57,000 (11%) of the victims were classified as children aged 0–14 years (Krug et al., 2002). Child death rates from each of the OECD countries were then compared with the national adult homicide rates (UNICEF, 2003). Correlations between the two rates were only discernible at the extremes: the analysis showed that the same small group of countries that had very low rates of child homicide also had very low rates of adult homicide, and the three nations with the highest child homicide rates – the US, Mexico and Portugal – also had significantly higher adult homicide rates. The bulk of the assessed countries, all with relatively low rates of child maltreatment fatality, showed variable rates of adult homicide. In this analysis, the New Zealand homicide rate for children aged 0–14 years between 1994 and 1998 was 1.3 per 100,000, compared with 2.5 per 100,000 for the population over 15 years of age. Using child and adult population figures for the period, this implies an average of 11 child and 71 adult homicides per year over that period. Child homicides constituted 13.5% of the total homicides for the same period. A recent study (Brookman & Nolan, 2006) indicates that children under 17 years of age constitute 13% of all homicide victims in England and Wales.

Who are the victims of child homicide?

Overall, very young children are killed more often than older children, and while some gender differences exist, these tend not to be significant. Ethnicity may also be a factor, although this has been shown to be associated with socioeconomic factors and to vary over time.

Age of victims

International research indicates that victims of child homicide are likely to be younger on average (2.8 years) than children reported to child protection services (average 7.2 years) (Pecora et al., 1992). In virtually every country, infants under 1 year of age have the highest rate of child homicide victimisation (UNICEF, 2003). Indeed, a recent study (Brookman & Nolan, 2006) indicates that this age group is the most highly victimised of the total population. In England and Wales, for example, children aged under 1 year had a victimisation rate of 6.3 per 100,000 children, compared with 3.3 for adults aged 24 years, the next highest victimisation age group.

The particular vulnerability of the very young child is illustrated in Table 2.1.

Another study found that homicide victim rates in the 0–4 age group were more than double those in the 5–14 age group (Krug et al., 2002). Children under 1 year of age have a risk level approximately three times that of children aged 1–4 years, who themselves face almost double the risk confronting children in the 5–14 age group (UNICEF, 2003). Data from the US for 2002 notes 41% of child victims of homicide were under 1 year of age (significantly higher than the 27% average throughout the 1990s), while children under 4 years of age accounted for 76% of the child homicide fatalities (NCCAN, 2004). Throughout the OECD countries as a whole, 24% of child homicides were of children under 1 year of age, and 55% were of children under

Table 2.1: Child maltreatment deaths in English-speaking countries during a five-year period in the 1990s (Australia, NZ and US 1994–1998; Canada and Ireland 1993–1997; and UK 1995–1999)

Country	Total deaths of children aged 0–14 years	Deaths of children under 1 year old	% of deaths under 1 year old
Australia	156	39	25
Canada	284	91	32
Ireland	12	4	33
New Zealand	55	19	34
United Kingdom	502	143	28
USA	7,081	1,889	27
TOTAL	8,090	2,185	27

Raw data extracted from
UNICEF Innocenti Report Card Issue No. 5, September 2003, p. 8.

5 years (UNICEF, 2003). A study in the US in 1984 found that the average age of child homicide victims was 3.3 years (American Humane Association cited in Armytage & Reeves, 1992).

All studies come to the same conclusion – in general, the risk of children becoming homicide victims declines with age, at least until early adolescence.

Gender and status in family

Unlike studies of sexual abuse, physical abuse studies have not detected any significant victim gender bias (NCCAN cited in Hansen, Conaway & Christopher, 1990), although slightly more boys than girls are homicide victims (Greenland cited in Armytage & Reeves, 1992; Pecora et al., 1992). Place and status in the family may be more significant than gender. For example, studies indicate that victims tend to be the youngest or only child in the household (Pecora et al., 1992).

Ethnicity

Surprisingly, in the studies reviewed here, few referred specifically to the ethnicity of child victims of homicide. However, a study from England and Wales (Brookman & Nolan, 2006), notes that black children were over-represented as victims of child homicide. An Australian study (Strang, 1996) found that Aboriginal children had higher rates of victimisation; and even these levels may have been understated because of the unreliability of the recording of ethnicity. In other studies (e.g. Nixon, Pearn, Wilkey & Petrie cited in Pecora et al., 1992), ethnic minority families have been found to be over-represented in child homicide statistics. Studies from the US also note that African American and Hispanic children entering adolescence (at around age 13) were becoming part of adult patterns of violent death at disproportionate rates (UNICEF, 2003).

What was the cause of death?

Among the homicides attributed to child abuse, studies reveal that the most common cause of death is injury to the head, followed by injuries to the abdominal area (Kotch et al., 1993; Krug et al., 2002). In 2000, data from 25 states in the US relating to 708 victims under 18 years of age, show that 54.5% of deaths were attributable to physical injury and 34.9% to neglect (UNICEF, 2003). However, in 2002, national data from the US revealed that of child maltreatment fatalities, 38% were attributed to neglect as the sole cause, 30% to physical abuse alone, and the remainder to multiple maltreatment or other maltreatment types (NCCAN, 2004). The recent study from England and Wales notes that in relation to the deaths of very young children there is a greater use of methods such as suffocation and shaking and an absence of any clear-cut injury that can be used to identify a specific method of killing (Brookman & Nolan, 2006). The cause of such deaths is, therefore, more open to debate.

Who are the perpetrators of child homicide?

The people who kill children tend to be known to the child, and while they have a number of characteristics in common, these cannot be used to identify potential homicide perpetrators as many other individuals share some or even many of these characteristics but are not at risk of committing child homicide. There are, however, a number of contributing factors that may increase the risk of a particular individual committing child homicide.

Child homicide is predominantly an intra-familial phenomenon (D'Orban, 1979; Stroud, 2000). In studies from the 1980s, most families involved in fatal maltreatment were two-parent households (Alfaro; Thompson & Wilson cited in Pecora et al., 1992). There is a growing awareness that different forms of violence in family situations can occur simultaneously. For example, it is important to note that an increasing body of evidence links spousal violence with violence towards children (Tomison, 2000).

Gender

An aspect of intra-familial child abuse that distinguishes it from other forms of violence relates to perpetrator gender. In general, men are considered to predominate as perpetrators and women as victims in most forms of interpersonal violent behaviour (Krug et al., 2002). With respect to child abuse and filicide[3], however, women feature more prominently as perpetrators, although still at a lesser rate than men (Howitt, 1992). This trend has been supported by an Australian study (New South Wales Child Protection Committee cited in Wilczynski, 1997), but the reverse has been found in an English study where perpetrators of child homicide are more likely to be women (Wilczynski, 1997). Contradictory findings occurred in US studies from the 1980s, some found the majority of child homicide perpetrators were biological fathers or de facto male partners (Alfaro; Thompson & Wilson cited in Pecora et al., 1992), while others identified mothers as the perpetrators in the majority of cases (Alfaro; Myers, Steele & Pollock). What is clear, however, is that female levels of offending begin to approach male levels in relation to very young children. This pattern is particularly evident in the study from England and Wales, which revealed almost equal numbers of male and females were perpetrators of child homicide (Brookman & Nolan, 2006). In an earlier study in England and Wales, 60% of the homicides of children under 1 year of age were committed by the mother (D'Orban, 1979).

In the US, reflecting a pattern that has remained consistent over time, one or both parents were involved in 79% of child homicides in 2002, while only 16% involved maltreatment by non-parental caregivers. The relationship of the perpetrator to the child in the remaining 5% of homicide cases was unknown or the data was missing (NCCAN, 2004). In the UK, filicide was estimated to constitute 71% of all child killings (Home Office cited in Wilczynski, 1997), with fathers being responsible for most deaths caused by physical abuse, while deaths caused by mothers were more likely to be associated with neglect (NCCAN, 2004). A further study from England and Wales reveals that biological parents, either male or female, were the killers of more than 70% of child homicide victims under 1 year of age (Brookman & Nolan, 2006).

Other characteristics

There is no single profile of a likely perpetrator of child homicide. However, studies of perpetrators of child abuse may provide some indication of possible commonalities. Several writers link child abuse perpetration with mental illness, others link it to a history of childhood abuse and to a number of stressors, including socioeconomic factors. Early studies into child abuse proposed that perpetrators exhibited severe psychopathology (Spinetta & Rigler, 1972). Walters (1975), however, proposed a much broader typology of abuse causation, which included social and parental incompetence, situational factors, and causation stemming from a perpetrator's experience of being a victim of abuse or mental illness. Belsky (1980) proposed that abusive parenting was best understood as the interplay between psychological disturbance in the adult, the presence of some characteristics in the children themselves that elicited an abusive response from their caregivers, problems in family functioning, social stressors, cultural contexts, and abuse-supportive values. This model is supported by evidence that emerged later (Kelly, 1990) suggesting that fewer abusive caregivers demonstrated diagnosable psychotic, schizophrenic, or sociopathic conditions. Rather, maltreatment incidents were related to complex interactions amongst a variety of parental traits, child characteristics, environmental influences, and stressors affecting the family.

More recent studies, however, clearly point to the existence of severe mental disturbance in some perpetrators. This leads to the proposition that mental illness may constitute a significant point of difference between those who kill and those who abuse children without fatal consequences (UNICEF, 2003). For example, a study of filicide in England and Wales (D'Orban, 1979) found that in 90% of cases that went before the courts, the perpetrator was considered to have a diagnosed psychiatric condition.

An aspect of debate in the literature relates to whether child homicide perpetrators are potentially identifiable from patterns of abusive behaviour prior to a fatality. However, the sheer number of what are described as 'single assault fatalities' challenges the widely held view that deaths result from gradually worsening levels of abuse or neglect (UNICEF, 2003). Such deaths may be characterised by contextual issues (such as a severe psychotic episode or a relationship breakdown) rather than by perpetrator behaviour that worsens over time. Family disputes were found to lead to the murder of children followed by the parent's suicide in just over a third (35%) of child homicides in Australia between 1989 and 1999 (Lawrence, 2004).

Studies from the US have found that homicide perpetrators tend to be younger on average than caregivers reported for non-fatal abuse, with the vast majority under 30 years of age (mean 26.7 years) (American Association for Protecting Children cited in Pecora et al., 1992). Ethnic minority and poor families tend to be over-represented in child fatalities (Nixon et al. cited in Pecora et al., 1992) and most perpetrators do not mean to kill or want to see their children die. Rather, death is the outcome of a series of unfortunate events (Mitchel cited in Pecora et al.,

Figure 2.1: Characteristics and events associated with perpetrators of child homicide

Perpetrator inside family		Perpetrator outside family
Women	Men who killed within the family	Men who killed outside the family

Characteristics associated with perpetrators:

Women
- Had children young (under 17), and in quick succession
- Did not access pre-natal care, or did so late in pregnancy
- Sole parent
- Socially isolated
- Victim of family violence as an adult
- Raised with harsh family discipline and parental strife
- History of suicide attempts or suicidal ideation

Men who killed within the family
- Poverty
- Low educational achievement
- Young
- Poor mental health, including alcohol or drug abuse
- Victim of family violence as a child
- Early offending
- Regularly unemployed
- Unemployed at time of killing
- Had been in state care
- Had more than three caregivers growing up
- Started using alcohol and drugs as a child
- History of offending as a child
- History of offending as an adult
- Being a stepfather
- In a de facto relationship
- History of abusing current or previous partners
- History of abusing children in their care
- History of abusing the child before killing

Men who killed outside the family
- Single at the time of killing
- History of violence to other children as a child
- Began offending young (before 12 years of age)
- Sexually abused as a child
- Convictions for serious and/or sexual assault

Events occurring in the perpetrator's life prior to child's death:

- Drinking or using drugs just before killing the child
- Relationship ending or fearing a relationship is ending
- Left to care for a young crying child
- Depressed
- Suicidal
- Psychotic

Adapted from Children at Increased Risk of Death from Maltreatment and Strategies for Prevention, *CYF & MSD, 2006, p. 20.*

1992). Where victims are under 1 year of age, female perpetrators kill male and female children in about the same proportion, but males are more likely to kill a male infant (Brookman & Nolan, 2006).

Certain characteristics of homicide perpetrator profiles continue to be identified; for example, youthfulness, low educational attainment, poverty, depression, and the existence of multiple stressors are common factors (NCCAN, 2004). There are cautions, though, about overemphasising the importance of individual factors, as Vondra (1990, p.151) notes:

> The truth is that every factor is embedded in an entire network of influences and each factor's relation to parenting is, in part, a consequence of its relations with many other relevant influences.

Child homicides perpetrated by strangers are not only less frequent but they have different characteristics to those found in intra-familial homicide. Victims are more likely to be older children in their teenage years, weapons are more likely to be involved, and the perpetrator is more likely to be male (Home Office cited in Wilczynski, 1997).

Figure 2.1 provides a summary of the common characteristics and events identified in the international literature as being associated with perpetrators of child death from maltreatment (Child, Youth and Family & Ministry of Social Development, 2006). It is important to note, however, that most people with some or even many of those characteristics never harm children. Individual and family resilience, access to timely, quality interventions, and other life opportunities can also reduce risk or remove it altogether. Factors overlap and interact, and the pathways to abuse are complex and varied.

While Figure 2.1 captures broadly the research findings, the way in which factors accumulate through the life course and reinforce each other can provide a richer understanding of risk.

Risk factors

Recent analysis of the literature (Child, Youth and Family & Ministry of Social Development, 2006) on perpetrators of child homicide shows

ure 2.2: Factors contributing to accumulated adversity for potential perpetrators: childhood, adulthood and immediate precursors

Childhood/adolescence	Adulthood	Immediate precursors
Females and males	**Females and males**	**Females and males**
Victim of family violence →	• Forming a relationship with physically abusive partner	• Family disputes and/or real or perceived threat of a relationship break-up
Aggressive offending before age 15	• In a de facto relationship	
Starts abusing drugs and alcohol	• Becoming parents at a young age	
	• Poor mental health, including drug and alcohol abuse →	• Poor mental health, including drug and alcohol abuse
Males	**Males**	
• Been in state care		**Males**
• Had more than 3 caregivers		
• Growing up in poverty	• Regularly unemployed →	• Unemployed
• Low academic attainment →	• History of offending	
• History of offending	• Been in prison	
	Males (killed child within family)	**Males (killed child within family)**
	• Abusing partner and children in their care	• Recent history of abusing the child killed
	• Stepfather	• Left to care for a young, crying child
Males (killed child outside family)	**Males (killed child outside family)**	
• Sexually abused →	• Sexual assault convictions	
• History of violence to other children	• Convictions for serious assault	
• Began offending young (before 12)		
Females	**Females**	**Females**
• Raised with harsh family discipline and parental strife	• Had a first child under 17, and subsequent children by 19 years	
	• No or late pre-natal care	
	• Sole parent	
	• Socially isolated →	• Socially isolated
	• History of suicide attempts or ideation	• Psychotic, depressed and/or suicidal

Death of a child from maltreatment

← ← ← ← ← ← ←

Reduction of risk from individual and family resilience, access to timely, quality interventions and/or economic and life opportunities

From CYF & MSD (2006, p. 21). Reproduced with permission.

the potential for risk factors to accumulate and reinforce other risk factors, and for childhood risk factors to trigger similar risk factors in adulthood. Hence the factors associated with increased risk of killing children can begin to accumulate in childhood, and then continue on into adulthood (see Figure 2.2).

As the factors accumulate, so they can trigger others over time. For example, if a child's early environment is characterised by family violence, this increases the potential for them to move into adult relationships that are also violent. Such risk factors can also be transferred across generations.

Related to the transfer of risk factors across generations is the ongoing debate regarding the relative influences of 'nature' and 'nurture' on the intergenerational transmission of violent behaviour.

The 'nature versus nurture' debate

Empirical evidence supporting the intergenerational transmission of abuse and violence has been quite weak (Fergusson, Boden & Horwood, 2006). However, recent research connected with the Dunedin longitudinal study of over a thousand children beginning in 1972 has found that aggressive behaviour in adulthood can be (but is not always) influenced by the interaction between genetic make-up and abusive or traumatic experience in childhood (Caspi, McClay, Moffitt, Mill, Martin, Craig, Taylor et al., 2002). When we experience danger or provocation we produce high levels of certain neurotransmitters that promote a hyper-aroused state, which enables us to respond appropriately – to fight, freeze or flee. Once the danger or provocation has past, enzymes (in particular MAOA) in the brain lower the levels of those neurotransmitters so that we can continue our life as normal.

The MAOA enzyme is produced by a gene which exists in alternative forms. These forms have varying levels of activity. Individuals with high-activity genes produce high levels of MAOA enzyme, and those with only low-activity genes produce low levels, which can leave them in a hyper-aroused state for an extended period of time. Which genes we possess is usually determined by what we inherit from both parents. This particular gene, though, is carried on the X chromosome. Because women have two X chromosomes, if they inherit a low-activity gene on one of their X chromosomes, then having a high-activity gene on their other X chromosome would compensate for it. It is trickier for men. Because men have only one X chromosome, if they inherit a single low-activity gene, then they will produce low levels of the MAOA enzyme, which would result in those men having sustained hyper-arousal.

What is most interesting about this research is that a low level of the MAOA enzyme by itself does not result in increased levels of aggressive behaviour. Increased levels of adult violence occur when low MAOA levels are combined with the experience of childhood trauma or abuse. The Dunedin study has found that abused children with low MAOA levels (12% of the people studied) accounted for 44% of the violent crimes committed by the whole group when they were adults. In addition, 85% of those males who had low MAOA levels and who were severely or moderately abused during childhood developed anti-social behaviour of some kind (Caspi et al., 2002). In contrast, Ridley (2003, pp. 267–8) notes:

> Remarkably, the ones with high-active MAOA genes were virtually immune to the effect of maltreatment. They did not get into trouble much even if maltreated as youngsters. Those with the low-active genes were much more anti-social if maltreated, and if anything slightly less anti-social than the average if not maltreated. The low-active maltreated men did four times their share of rapes, robberies and assaults.

Hence in Figure 2.3 we can see the impact of an important interaction between genetic make-up (nature) and upbringing (nurture).

The fact that the gene is carried on the X chromosome is also interesting with respect to differing levels of male and female violence in the general population. Women, having the extra X chromosome, would need to inherit two of the low-activity genes to become more susceptible to the long-term effects of childhood abuse, and the probability of inheriting two low-activity genes is much less than that of inheriting just one.

Figure 2.3: Effect of gene–environment interaction on aggressive behaviour in adults

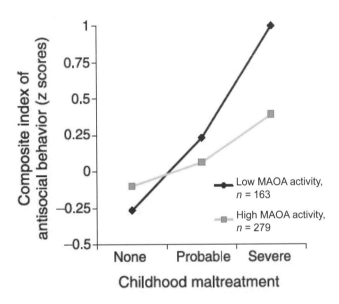

From Caspi et al. (2002, p. 851), reproduced with permission.

As this work develops it is likely to offer new insights into the relationship between childhood abuse and subsequent adult violence. However, it is important to note that while this research provides a significant perspective on why some adults are violent towards their children, it can only provide part of the explanation. It may explain why some abused children become adults who go on to abuse their own children, while others who were also abused in childhood do not. It does not explain why some non-abused children go on to abuse their own children, or why some people who were abused as children and have low levels of MAOA refrain from abusing their children. It is important, however, that we more fully understand this research and consider its implications across the range of disciplines working with children who are abused. According to Stokstad (2002, p. 752), it has the potential to 'lead to better intervention strategies'. It also raises important issues with respect to prevention.

Prior involvement of child care and protection authorities

Internationally there is often agency involvement with child homicide victims and their families prior to a child's death:

> What disturbs many child welfare professionals and child advocates is that a substantial number of these families [in which fatalities have occurred] had been reported to or served by [child protection services] at least once before the child's death. (Pecora et al., 1992, p. 111)

It could be argued that given the links between child abuse and other family problems, one might expect a significant involvement of child care and protection authorities in cases where children have died of neglect or physical assault. International studies confirm this. In a UK study, a high proportion of filicidal parents (79.5%) had been seen on a number of occasions prior to a child's homicide by a variety of helping professionals (Block & Tilton cited in Wilczynski, 1997). A lower proportion (59%) was claimed for Australian cases (NSWCPC cited in Wilczynski, 1997). A study from the US found that of the children who died from abuse or neglect annually, almost half were known to child protection agencies before their deaths because of their family situations and the risks these presented to the child (Costin et al. cited in Stoesz, 2002). Earlier US studies indicated that 25% of child homicides occurred in families known to agencies providing social services (Armytage & Reeves, 1992). In both the UK and Australian studies the most common reason for agency contact was the mental health of a parent (Wilczynski, 1997). Definitional and counting issues, however, have the potential to impact on the usefulness of these comparisons. For example, reports from the US relate to contacts with child protection agencies, while reports from the UK include a wider range of agencies.

A small New Zealand study (Kinley & Doolan, 1997) of five child homicides found that all of the children had been referred to child-welfare authorities. In four of the five cases there had been two or more referrals, and in one case there had been five referrals. Concerns about possible physical abuse, however, were given as the reason for referral in only two cases. This accentuates the need for careful analysis of reported concerns about children, even where patterns of family violence may not be the presenting issue.

Although this small study suggests that New Zealand may follow international patterns with respect to families having previous statutory involvement, as we shall see in Chapter 3, as few as 20% of the child homicides during the five-year period 1996 to 2000 involved children who were known to Child, Youth and Family. The results of the New Zealand study, therefore, contrast strongly with those from Australia, the US, and the UK, which cite rates from 59% to 80%. Instead they are closer to the findings of another Australian study of child homicide cases which found that only one in four families had experienced prior contact with child protection authorities (Armytage & Reeves, 1992).

We will return to this issue in Chapter 6 where we look at the New Zealand child homicide data for the 1996–2000 period and examine more closely the cases of the small number of children who were known to Child, Youth and Family prior to their deaths. In Chapter 3, however, we will focus on recorded data relating to the group of 91 New Zealand child homicide victims who died in the decade 1991–2000 and compare the findings with those of international studies.

Notes

[2] 'When no other cause or motive can be established, the death of a child is most likely to be the result of abuse or neglect that cannot be proved in a court of law' (UNICEF, 2003, p. 7).

[3] Defined as death of a child caused by a biological parent of the child.

Chapter 3

Child homicide in New Zealand

There are significant gaps in our knowledge and understanding of the child homicide phenomenon in New Zealand. There have been few attempts to understand the prevalence and nature of fatal violence towards children and to identify which children are most at risk and from whom. Most of what is known in New Zealand about child death by homicide has been taken from international literature, with local writers providing some commentary on the implications of the literature for this country (Ridley & Scott, 1999; Wilson, 1997). Studies undertaken in New Zealand in the early 1990s have provided an analysis of morbidity and death due to child abuse (Kotch et al., 1993) and attempted to identify homicide patterns related to children who were known to New Zealand child-protection authorities (Kinley & Doolan, 1997).

In this chapter we look at what official records can tell us about rates of child homicide in New Zealand over time. While actual numbers of deaths remained relatively stable over the period 1978–2000, there have been significant changes in the rates of homicide within different ethnic groups over that period. Because police statistics provide a rich source of data, we then look more closely at police data relating to children who died from maltreatment in New Zealand between 1991 and 2000. We chose this time frame for a more in-depth study because we were able to access data from records kept by Child Youth and Family relating to children who had died and were known to the agency for at least some of that period. As we noted in Chapter 1, this data began to be collected in a systematic way from 1994, offering an opportunity for an analysis that may help us to understand more of the history of the children who died.

In a close examination of the data recorded by the New Zealand Police and Child, Youth and Family, we look at the characteristics of children whose lives were cut short by violence, and those of the people who are responsible for their deaths. But first we need to discuss the reporting and recording issues relating to child homicides.

Reporting and recording patterns

Because police data are not necessarily collected for the purposes of research, there are some inevitable limitations in terms of the scope of the information that is recorded. For example, when child homicides occur no information is recorded relating to the characteristics of the perpetrator, such as age, the circumstances of the family, and levels of income or employment. The data do not capture the history of previous family violence incidents, nor information relating to mental health issues. Essentially, the data record characteristics of the child (age, gender, ethnicity, and cause of death) and a limited amount of detail related to the perpetrator (gender, relationship to child, and method used to cause the death). The analysis of the data is thus limited to the information police are required to record and we have therefore not been able to compare key demographic factors concomitant with child homicide that feature in the international literature. Further study would be required to determine trends associated with perpetrators' age, financial, employment, or mental health status, or whether the homicides are linked to other forms of violence in households.

While one might assume that the recording of child death by homicide will be a straightforward process of counting, this is not necessarily the case. Part of the problem relates to how we define child homicide. We take it to mean the killing of a child by a deliberate act of violence or negligence, irrespective of whether the perpetrator intended to kill the child. To ensure we had as full a set of data as possible of all children known to have died from deliberate violence or negligence we supplemented police records for the period 1996–2000 with those of Child, Youth and Family. We found two omissions in the recording of this official data. The literature indicates that time delays can affect the identification of deaths as homicide, and some homicides escape entry into official data records entirely.

Of the 91 homicides that occurred between 1991 and 2000 only two were attributed to neglect. The neglect rate of 2.2% of all child homicides contrasts strongly with rates of up to 38% recorded in the US. It is likely, as noted in Chapter 2, that deaths from neglectful supervision (as distinct from withholding essential life-supporting resources), such as drowning, house fires, or being run over in a household driveway, have been included in those statistics, in contrast to the New Zealand situation where they are excluded from official statistics on child homicide. It is also possible that the issue of whether or not those kinds of child deaths result in a criminal prosecution of the neglectful caregiver may have some bearing on the classification of the death as homicide or accidental death. In the US, as a result of child-mortality review processes, there has been an increase in the total number of homicides identified as the result of neglect. Similar processes have been established in New Zealand under the auspices of the Ministry of Health, and future studies may also map the influence of this process on maltreatment death statistics.

The matter of deaths due to neglectful supervision is probably an area where definitional issues are most debated. Sympathy and concern for otherwise caring and responsible parents who have had a lapse in concentration that resulted in the death of their child render it difficult to attribute such deaths to culpable negligence, let alone categorise them as homicides. Child mortality review systems will need to grapple with the issue of definition and ensure the definitions that are adopted enhance the ability of one country to compare its performance against that of other countries, or at least explain variations better.

Child homicide rates in New Zealand

To gain a sense of the changes in the rate of child homicide that have occurred over time, we looked at two periods: 1978–1987 and 1991–2000. Data for the 1991–2000 period are from police records and are likely to be of a high quality. Data for the 1978–1987 period are from the findings of another study (Kotch et al., 1993) that was based on information gleaned from records kept by health authorities. The latter study did not provide the raw data, although it noted that it had included some deaths that were clearly homicides, but which were not identified on the health records as deaths resulting from child battering or other maltreatment (Kotch et al., 1993). This raises the possibility that some of these misdiagnosed deaths neither achieved homicide status nor were they processed by the criminal justice system. Thus the 1978–1987 health data may be more accurate than police data for the same period.

Overall, national child homicide statistics appear to have changed little when we compare the two periods. Comparisons are made on the basis of the number of deaths relative to the general resident child population aged 0–14 years, based on New Zealand census data. During the period 1978–1987, the mean number of child homicides was 7.7 per year (0.94 deaths per 100,000 children aged 0–14 per year). During the period 1991–2000, the mean number of child homicides was 9.1 deaths per year (1.07 per 100,000 children per year).

In terms of ethnic identity, however, the statistics reveal a significant difference in how the homicide rates for Māori and non-Māori children changed when comparing the two periods, with an increased death rate for Māori children and a decreased rate for non-Māori children. During the period 1978–1987, the mean number of Māori child homicides was 1.4 per year (1.05 per 100,000 per year) but by the period 1991–2000 it had risen to 4.7 per year (2.40 per 100,000 per year). By comparison, there was a decrease in the mean number of non-Māori child homicides from 6.3 per year for 1978–1987 (0.92 per 100,000 per year) to 4.4 per year for 1991–2000 period (0.67 per 100,000 per year), as shown in Figure 3.1.

Figure 3.1: Mean child homicide rates (per 100,000 population aged 0–14 years per year)

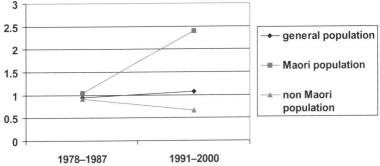

For the period 1978–1987 the difference between the mean child homicide rates for Māori (1.05 per 100,000 per year) and non-Māori (0.92) is not statistically significant. However, for the period 1991–2000 the difference between the Māori rate (2.40 per 100,000 per year) and non-Māori rate (0.67) is highly significant. The increase in the Māori rate across the two time-frames (from 1.05 to 2.40 per 100,000 per year) is also highly significant. The decrease in the non-Māori rate across the two time-frames (from 0.92 to 0.67 per 100,000 per year) is significant.

This means that while the overall rate of child homicide in the general population has remained relatively constant over time, there have been notable changes in the rates for Māori and non-Māori populations. A slight fall in the rate of non-Māori child homicide victimisation was offset by a large increase in the victimisation rate for Māori children. However, while Māori child homicide deaths were 52% of all child homicide deaths over the 1990s decade, there was a concentration of Māori deaths in the earlier part of that decade. Māori deaths accounted for 59% of all child homicide deaths between 1991 and 1995, but only 44% between 1996 and 2000. Preliminary comment on the figures for the next 5-year period 2001–2005 (Doolan, 2006) indicates that this downward trend is being maintained. While the police data made available in 2006 must be viewed with caution because of their recency and thus greater potential unreliability, they do show that the overall numbers of Māori child homicides are falling, as shown in Figure 3.2.

Over this 15-year period the proportion of all child homicides that involve Māori victims is also falling, as shown in Figure 3.3.

However, it should be noted that during the 2001–2005 period ethnicity was recorded as unknown in one case and this case was included with non-Māori data in this later analysis. Should this homicide case subsequently prove to involve a Māori victim, the Māori proportion of all child homicides for the period 2001–2005 would be similar to that of the previous five-year period (1996–2000) – such is the impact of a single reclassification on the small numbers involved. Even in that event, however, a decrease in the rate of Māori child homicide over the past decade can be seen when compared with the period 1991–1995.

The data for the non-Māori population included Samoan and Asian sub-populations. A further examination of the data provides a

Figure 3.2: Māori child homicide numbers in three five-year periods between 1991 and 2005

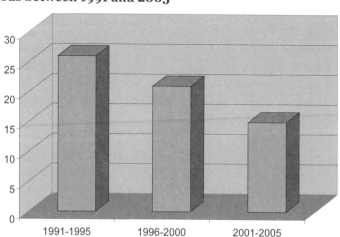

measure of homicide rates for Pacific Island groups. During the decade 1991–2000, the mean homicide rate for the Samoan population aged 0–14 years was of 0.76 per 100,000 per year. The data provides no evidence of homicide victimisation for children of the six other major Pacific populations – Cook Islander, Fijian, Niuean, Tokelauan, Tongan and Tuvaluan – whose combined New Zealand resident populations equal that of the Samoan people.[4] However, this is not so for the Asian child population, where a mean homicide rate of 0.92 per 100,000 children per year has been recorded.[5] The distribution of child homicides rates across ethnic groups is shown in Table 3.1.

It is important to exercise caution when considering homicide statistics relating to ethnicity. As we noted in Chapter 2, the small numbers involved and the consequent volatility of child death statistics mean that even more care is needed when disaggregating the data into ethnic groups.

In summary, the available statistics show that, on average, nine children died each year as a result of homicide during the period 1991–

Figure 3.3: Changes in the proportions of Māori and non-Māori child homicides over three five-year periods between 1991 and 2005

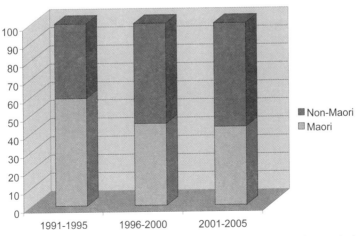

From Doolan (2006, p. 25), reproduced with permission.

Table 3.1: Child homicide rates across ethnic groups 1991–2000

Ethnic group	Mean annual population of 0–14-year-olds	Mean homicide rate per 100,000 children per year
Māori	196,406	2.40
Asian	43.196	0.92
Samoan	39,408	0.76
Pākehā[6]	531,226	067
Other Pacific	38,357	0.00
Total population	**846,593**	**1.07**

2000, which represents a mean rate of 1.07 children per 100,000 child population per year, or 0.24 children per 100,000 of the total general population resident in New Zealand per year. How does this compare with international child homicide rates?

International comparisons

The repeated cautions in the literature about reporting and counting issues in relation to child homicide render inter-country comparisons and relative positions questionable. The UNICEF (2003) study for the period 1994–1998 recorded a child maltreatment mortality rate for New Zealand of 1.20 per 100,000 children per year, while our research calculated the mean mortality rate as 1.02 per 100,000 for the same period. Thus, either the New Zealand police data were incomplete compared with data available to the UNICEF study and therefore represent an undercounting of actual child maltreatment mortality cases, or the disparity represents the difference between the raw data used in this study and the weighted data used by UNICEF. What can be said is that New Zealand has a reported child maltreatment mortality rate higher than that reported by most countries within the developed world, and that its position relative to these countries has deteriorated since the early 1970s. Offsetting that to some extent is the fact that New Zealand has a lower level of deaths classified as 'of undetermined intent' than countries such as the UK, France, the US, Canada, and Japan, which are therefore likely to be under-reporting their child deaths due to maltreatment. The undercounting of deaths that may arise from neglect both in New Zealand and internationally creates additional problems in terms of understanding incidence. Whether adding these would worsen New Zealand's position is difficult to determine given the high level of generality of the UNICEF report data and the lack of any common definition of homicide used by countries within the OECD.

Child homicide statistics 1991–2000

We now look more closely at the New Zealand police statistics for the period 1991–2000, when a total of 91 children died as a result of homicide and 101 perpetrators were involved in the deaths of these children.

Age distribution

An examination of the data reveals some interesting patterns in terms of the age distribution of children who were killed in this period (see Figure 3.4). Younger children are more likely to become victims of homicide than older children. Out of the total sample of 91 child homicides, 75 (82%) involved children under 10 years of age. The higher number of children in the under-5 age bracket is particularly notable as these 57 children made up almost two-thirds (63%) of the homicide victims. The high number of children who became homicide victims in the first year of their lives is even more striking. These 24 children constituted a quarter (26%) of all child homicides. The remaining 16 children (18%) were aged 11–14 years. While the average age of victims was 4.5 years, there are differences between the two main ethnic categories: the average age of Māori child homicide victims was 3.7 years, and that of non-Māori, 5.4 years. The average age of the 82 children killed by someone known to them was 3.9 years

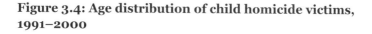

Figure 3.4: Age distribution of child homicide victims, 1991–2000

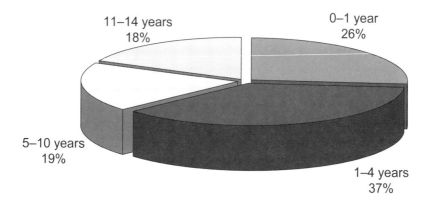

but the average age of the five children killed by strangers was 11.8 years (in four cases the relationship to the child was not recorded).

The findings that child homicide victims are more likely to be under 5 years of age than over, and that they are more likely to be under 1 year of age than any other age, are consistent with the international literature. However, the average age at death of 4.5 years is higher than overseas studies have found (a range of 2.8 [Pecora et al., 1992] to 3.3 years [AHA cited in Armytage & Reeves, 1992]). This is largely due to the somewhat higher than average age at death for non-Māori children as compared with Māori children. The average age at death for Māori children is only marginally above international comparisons. That the average age of children killed by strangers is generally much higher than those killed by caregivers is supported by this study.

The high proportion of child homicide victims under the age of 5 years (63%, n = 57) may be related to a number of factors. For example, the period between birth and entry to school can be a time of isolation from professional helping sources. This is particularly so if the child is not attending pre-school, is not seen by a health professional, or, alternatively, is seen by a number of different health professionals who have no means of checking information with one another. These factors can be seen in the tragic death of James Whakaruru in 1999 that attracted intense political and public attention in New Zealand. The inquiry into James's death (Office of the Commissioner for Children [OCC], 2000) found that during his four years of life, James had contact with at least 40 health professionals, sometimes as a result of what we now know to have been non-accidental injuries. However, rarely did the same professional see him more than a few times and there was no system for information sharing between health professionals.

There is no effective way of monitoring the safety and well-being of all children under 5 years of age apart from the vigilance of the extended family, friends and neighbours, as well as those educational and health professionals who have some contact with the children. Furthermore, since the abolition of the Family Benefit in 1990, there is no national database in New Zealand that records the whereabouts of all children and their families. The mobility of some at-risk families can prevent communities and local professionals from developing a picture of a child and his or her network of support. Indeed, there is some evidence that families in which abuse is occurring avoid outside contacts through a phenomenon described as closure. Reder, Duncan and Gray (1993, p. 99) provide a description of how this process prevents children from receiving adequate care and protection:

> This was a striking phenomenon noted in over half of the thirty-five cases, in which the family attempted to tighten the boundary around them so that they reduced their contact with the external world and few people were able to meet or speak with them. For example, their curtains were always drawn, the children stopped playing outside and no longer attended school or nursery. The parents failed [to attend] appointments with professionals, the children were not taken to scheduled visits to health clinics and social workers and health visitors could not obtain entry to the home when they called.

All of this reinforces the importance of professionals having a common understanding of the particular vulnerabilities of pre-school children and the need to work together to enhance the safety/support network around an at-risk child. Enabling greater information sharing amongst professionals has the potential to increase opportunities to provide protection for those at risk.

Children under 1 year of age are more likely to become child homicide victims (26% of the study group) than children of any other age. This is likely to relate to factors such as their physical vulnerability, their total dependence on adults, and their capacity to cry incessantly and drive an exhausted/enraged parent to act in ways that they normally would not, by shaking a baby, for example. This means that workers need to be especially vigilant when safety concerns have been raised in relation to infants.

Gender

Our examination of the data revealed that boys were slightly more at risk of homicide than girls: 48 victims were male (53%) and 42 female (46%). The gender of one, an unborn child, was unknown (see Figure 3.5).

This pattern is consistent with the international literature, which reveals that the homicide victimisation rate for boys is marginally higher than that for girls.

Figure 3.5: Gender of child homicide victim 1991–2000

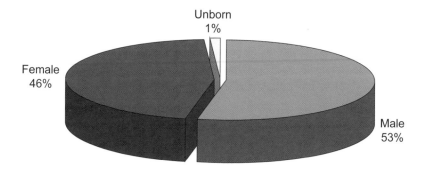

The New Zealand Police data do not include further information, such as the number of children in the family or the child's position relative to other children. Hence it is not possible to know whether a homicide victim was the only child in a family, had siblings, or was the youngest in the family.

Ethnicity

As we have seen within the 1991–2000 sample, Māori made up the greatest proportion of children who were victims of homicide, a total of 47 children (52%), followed by 35 Pākehā children (39%). Of the remaining 9 children (9%), 4 were Asian, 3 Samoan and the ethnicity of 2 children was not recorded (see Figure 3.6).

The relationship between the proportion of victims belonging to different ethnic groups and the distribution of ethnicity across the total child population is illustrated in Table 3.2.

Clearly in child homicide victimisation figures Māori are significantly over-represented when considered in the context of the total child population. However, recent data indicates that this is changing. Whereas in the ten-year period 1991–2000 the Māori rate was more than 3.5 times that of the non-Māori rate, for the period

Figure 3.6: Ethnicity of child homicide victims, 1991–2000

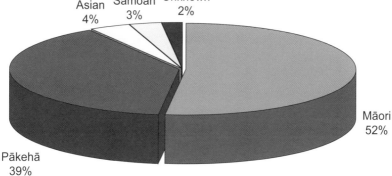

Table 3.2: Proportion of child homicide deaths by ethnicity compared with proportion of child population 0–14 years by ethnicity, 1991–2000

Ethnicity	% of child homicide victims	% of all children aged 0–14 years
Pākehā	38.5	65.2
Māori	51.6	23.1
Asian	4.4	5.0
Samoan	3.3	4.7
Other Pacific	0.0	4.7
Unknown	2.2	0.0
Total	**100.00**	**100.00**

2001–2005 the Māori rate was somewhere between 2.3 and 2.5 times that of the non-Māori rate (the range reflecting the fact that one child's ethnicity was not recorded) (Doolan, 2006). We return to this issue later in the chapter.

Cause of death

Data relating to the cause of death provide further information about the types of violence that contribute to the deaths of children (see Figure 3.7). Here again there were some differences according to ethnic groupings in our study. Head injuries contributed to the deaths of 30 children, the largest group of child victims (33%); 13 had injuries to other body parts (14%); 18 died from stab wounds, a cut throat, or bleeding to death (20%); 17 from strangulation, asphyxiation or suffocation (19%); of the remaining 13 children (14%), five died from poisoning, three from drowning, two from neglect, and two from gunshot wounds, while in one case the cause of death was unknown or not recorded.

All but two of the homicides involved forms of physical violence, as opposed to acts of omission or neglect.

Figure 3.7: Cause of death

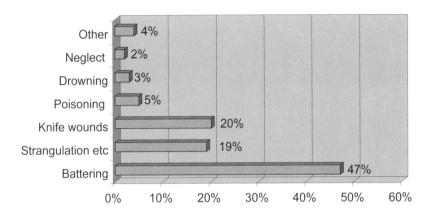

The pattern of injuries causing death also conforms to that found in international studies, with the largest group, comprising one-third of cases, involving head injuries. This should be regarded as a minimum figure as many records gave the cause of death in more general terms, such as 'multiple physical injuries', which may have also included injury to the head.

Child homicide as a proportion of all homicides

Although the proportion of child homicides to all homicides during the 1991–2000 period was small, this level appears to be a little higher than international averages. Our examination of the data reveals that child homicide averaged 15.2% of all homicides in New Zealand over the 1991–2000 decade. The range was from a low of 5.7% in 2000 to a high of 25% in 1999 (see Figure 3.8). During the decade, census statistics show that the proportion of children in the total New Zealand population averaged 23% (New Zealand census data 1991 and 1996).

At 15%, the average proportion of child homicides is slightly higher than an apparent international average of 11%, but it is difficult to know whether there is any significance in the difference given the high level of generality of the international figures.

Figure 3.8: Child homicide as a proportion of all homicides, 1991–2000

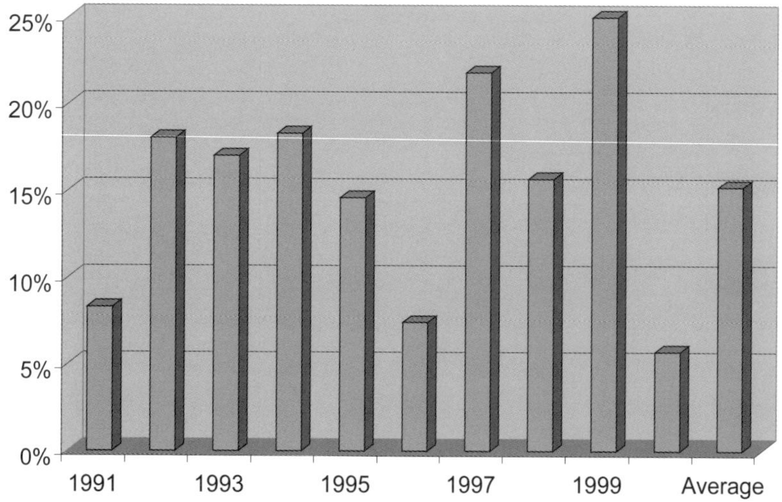

Given the over-representation of Māori children in the child homicide statistics, it is important for us to have an understanding of the significance of the differences between average child homicide rates for Māori and non-Māori populations. The Māori child homicide rate of 2.4 per 100,000 Māori child population per year parallels the child homicide rate of the US, which in turn has one of the highest general population homicide rates in the industrialised world. If the international pattern, where high rates of child homicide reflect high rates of general population homicide, holds true, then the high rate of homicide for Māori children ought to reflect a high rate of homicide for Māori generally. An examination of the homicide figures more generally indicates that this is indeed the case in New Zealand (Fanslow, Chalmers & Langley, 1995).

The perpetrators

There were a total of 101 perpetrators involved in the deaths of the 91 children – seven children were killed by two perpetrators and one child was killed by four persons. Our analysis is based on 101 homicidal acts and reveals a number of factors that can broaden our understanding of the people who kill children.

Gender

There were twice as many male perpetrators (67) as there were female (34) (see Figure 3.9).

Figure 3.9: Gender of child homicide perpetrators, 1991–2000

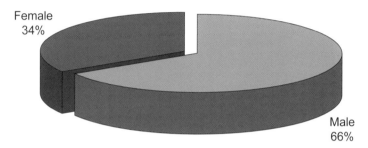

Although the number of men was far greater than the number of women, any perception that women are more likely to be passive perpetrators, or more likely to be involved with deaths resulting from neglect, is not supported by the findings of this study. Conversely, women recorded a lower use of battering than men (29% of women sole perpetrators as opposed to 56% of men). Conversely, women employed methods such as suffocation, asphyxiation or strangulation at a much higher rate (46% of women as opposed to 9% of men). Men used other means of killing, such as drowning, poisoning, stabbing or allowing a child to bleed to death, at a greater rate (35%) than women (25%). The findings reinforce the fact that no assumptions can be made with respect to gender. Both men and women are capable of violence towards their young.

Relationship to victim

The 1991-2000 police data also provide some information about the relationship between the perpetrator and the child (see Figure 3.10).

Figure 3.10: The relationship of perpetrators to child homicide victims, 1991–2000

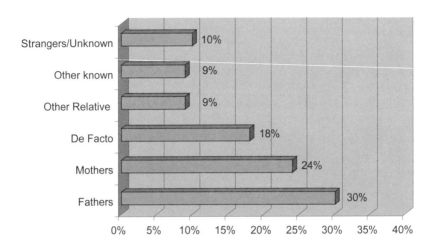

The results of the analysis support international findings that in the majority of cases perpetrators of child homicide are likely to be known to the child. Our analysis shows that 31 were biological fathers, the largest group of perpetrators, and 24 were biological mothers. The next largest group was made up of 18 de facto partners of a parent, followed by nine who were related to the child, and a similar group of nine who were unrelated but knew the child, including one boarder, two neighbours, four acquaintances, and two non-family caregivers. The remaining group of ten was made up of six strangers and four people whose relationship to the child was either not known or not recorded. Here again differences were found between cases involving Māori and non-Māori children. De facto partners were involved in the deaths of 16 Māori children (34% of all Māori homicide victims) and the deaths of only two non-Māori children (6%).

In the 52 cases where the death was classified as filicide, 55 parents were involved, 28 perpetrators were fathers (54%), 21 were mothers (40%), while in three cases the mother and father acted jointly (6%) as shown in Figure 3.11.

In the 24 homicides where the child was under 1 year of age, 15 of the deaths (63%) were due to filicide. There were equal numbers of paternal and maternal perpetrators of infanticide, and in one case the child's parents acted jointly. For the remaining nine children in this age group, the perpetrator was someone known to the child (37%).

Quite clearly perpetrators knew the child victims in all but a handful of the 91 cases that we examined. This confirms the findings of overseas studies that child homicide is predominantly an intra-familial phenomenon.

In cases of filicide, women appear to be equally as likely as men to be perpetrators of infanticide, but over the total age range, however, fathers tend to be twice as likely as mothers to be perpetrators of child homicide. This is entirely consistent with the literature.

While the proportion of deaths attributed to de facto partners is relatively low, overall (19.7%), there is a marked difference in the cases of Māori and non-Māori children, as we saw earlier. De facto partners were the perpetrators of the deaths of 16 Māori children but only two non-Māori children. However, because the numbers are low and there is a lack of more detailed information, it is difficult to draw any conclusions from this. Patterns of cohabitation differ across cultures and over time and cultural differences need to be explored more fully

Figure 3.11: Filicide perpetrators, 1991–2000

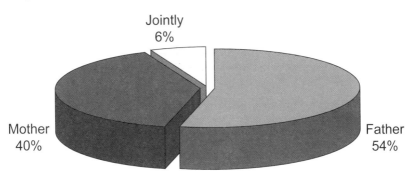

in context. It does, nevertheless, signal the need for research attention in this area.

Multiple homicides and murder–suicides

During the period under study, there appear to have been at least eight multiple homicide incidents, involving 20 children in total. The apparent number of multiple homicides (inferred from groupings of children killed by the same method by the same perpetrator on the same day) raises a number of questions. It is possible that these represent cataclysmic family events, and may be associated with the occurrence of adult relationship break-up or a dispute between parents over questions of custody of and access to children following family dissolution.[7] Such events are not associated with multiple homicides only and may well be linked to individual child homicides. Unfortunately we were not able to identify any such cases because of the limitations of the data.

Murder–suicide in the context of the parents' relationship ending has been noted in the international literature. In a UK study, for example, researchers found that in a third of the murder–suicide cases there was no evidence of any previous abuse of the children, the deaths being linked with the threat of the parents' relationship ending (Cavanagh, Emerson Dobash & Dobash, 2005). Australian researchers found that just over a third of child homicides were followed by the perpetrator parent's suicide (Lawrence, 2004).

This is a significantly underdeveloped area of research in New Zealand. If we are to better understand child homicide, it is important that we look further into the phenomenon of multiple homicide, and also the issues associated with murder–suicide where parents kill children and then themselves. These situations are relatively rare and thus studies and findings are restricted by low sample numbers. Nevertheless, one small study by Pritchard (2001) has explored filicide in the context of dispute between parents who have separated. The case study analysis investigated six Australian/New Zealand cases occurring between 1994 and 2000 in which a parent completed or attempted suicide after killing their children. All three of the New Zealand cases were filicides followed by suicides, and two of the three involved multiple child deaths – three children in each family. Two of the New Zealand perpetrators were male and had a history of violence towards their partners but neither had a history of child physical abuse.

Ethnicity, age and vulnerability

As we have noted, there are difficulties in analysing the victim data by ethnicity, and there are no police data on perpetrator ethnicity. Nevertheless, our findings raise some concerns about the particular vulnerability of Māori children. Placed in an international context, UNICEF's (2003) cross-nation study found that while ethnic minorities often have higher levels of child maltreatment, '[I]t seems likely that the operative factor is not ethnicity but poverty (which disproportionately affects ethnic minority families' (p. 16).

No discussion on differences between the rates for Māori and non-Māori should ignore the underlying differences in socioeconomic status. Māori are more likely to experience the socioeconomic factors associated with increased risk of death from child maltreatment. In addition, it is important to note that the effects of the economic reforms in New Zealand during the 1980s and 1990s have arguably created a significantly disadvantaged group that has disproportionately included Māori (Cheyne, O'Brien & Belgrave, 1997). While it is difficult to distinguish the contribution of social disadvantage from that of other factors, it is clear that in the particular period under study Māori were disadvantaged across a range of aspects:

> Changes in the economic climate over the past 15 years have had a major impact on the Māori population. This is shown in higher rates of unemployment and growing differences in income between Māori and non-Māori. (MSD, 2002, p. 73)

In any comparison of the living standards and social well-being of Māori and Pākehā, Māori as a group fare less well.

Protective factors mitigating child abuse include strong social ties and community support systems. It is likely that the 'community' in which some Māori families now live is in reality a collection of strangers. There has been a loss of civil society for some urban Māori who once interacted with the social structure and collectivity of whānau, hapū, iwi. It may be that the modelling of values, customs and beliefs underpinning life, family, care of children and social behaviour is less and less visible to young Māori families and to families more generally.

In summary, a total of 91 child deaths in New Zealand during the decade under study (1991–2000) were classed as homicides, an average of nine children per year.[8] While the greatest proportion of the child homicides was of children under 10 years of age (82%), the large proportions of children under 5 years (63%) and under 1 year of age (26%) clearly indicates that younger children are more vulnerable and infants most vulnerable to fatal injury from a violently abusive adult. These findings alone reinforce the need for practitioners to pay particular attention to the vulnerability of young children and infants when they are notified to professional social service agencies, such as child protection and health systems. Generally unable to protect themselves and having less robust bodies, they are more likely to be seriously injured when abused by an adult. Communicating this message to parents through established universal services for families with young children may well have longer-term benefits in this regard. We return to this discussion in the final chapter of the book.

When it comes to developing an understanding of child homicide based on research findings, it is important to realise that the findings are inevitably shaped by the data that was available to be studied – in this study the data was primarily demographic characteristics collected by police after a homicide had occurred. Different data sets may well generate alternative understandings. In the absence of other demographic descriptors, one variable such as race or ethnicity might achieve ascendancy as a risk factor in child homicide that is not fully justified. For example, Pryor and Rodgers (2001) have established seven factors influencing the social, psychological and physical development of children: family social class and income, family environmental factors (such as violence, for example), parental mental states, family criminality, stressful life events, social supports from significant others, and neighbourhood characteristics. Had the police also collected demographic data relating to these factors, for example, different variables contributing to increased levels of homicide risk may have emerged. To understand which of these, or combinations of these, contribute most to the risk of child homicide requires analysis of data that is not currently available. While it is probably unrealistic to expect police to collect this sort of information for research purposes, child mortality review processes are able to access a range of data relating to children who have died as a result of homicide. This may provide greater opportunities to explore more fully the range of factors that impact on child homicide, including ethnicity.

In the first part of this book, we explored the research, both international and national, relating to child homicide. We now explore the ways in which we respond to children who die from maltreatment.

Notes

[4] The 1995 data lists one victim as Polynesian, and this death has been included with non-Māori data but cannot be ascribed further. The child could have been Māori, Samoan, or from any other Pacific population.

[5] Population figures are based on 1991, 1996, and 2001 census data from Statistics NZ and have been averaged.

[6] Pākehā is the term used for New Zealand children of European decent. Numbers were calculated as total population minus Asian, Māori, and all Pacific nation sub-populations.

[7] There are, of course, other possible explanations. The murder of the Aplin children, outside the period of this study, followed a disclosure of child sexual abuse (OCC, 2003).

[8] This average fell to seven per year for the period 2001–2005 (Doolan, 2006).

Chapter 4

Responding to the deaths of children

Although child deaths resulting from battery or other assaults are rare in terms of the total population of children, the impact of a child dying in this way is felt far beyond the child's own family context. These deaths touch a deep vein of public emotion and often trigger a media frenzy, followed by a public outcry, calls for accountability, and expectations of statutory reform. The first significant child homicide death review undertaken in the UK in 1973 was triggered by such a case. The tragic death of young Maria Colwell brought child homicide to the forefront of public attention. Maria was seven years old when she was killed by her step-father. She had been looked after by foster parents for a number of years before her death, but had been returned to her mother and step-father's care when they successfully applied for custody through the court. The review of the circumstances surrounding her death was highly critical of the UK child welfare system and its capacity to keep Maria safe. Since Maria's death, reviews of high-profile tragedies have become a common response in English-speaking countries.

Despite their rarity, child death reviews have tended to shape international understandings of child abuse more generally and have been influential with respect to professional systems of response. Within the current climate it is possible for the death of a single child to result in calls for widespread child welfare reform (Ferguson, 2004).

Although it is clearly important that we understand the circumstances surrounding a particular child's death, it is wrong to assume that one tragic situation necessarily characterises practice with children and families across an entire system. Indeed, such rare events are just as likely to reflect a set of idiosyncratic circumstances located in a particular time and place.

In this chapter, then, we explore the impact of child death reviews and how using child death reviews as the key mechanism for understanding risk for children has unintended consequences – it has the potential to create risk-averse practices. The risk-averse system that this process unintentionally fosters may ultimately harm more children than it protects. However, before we explore these issues in detail we briefly discuss how the safety of children has been managed over time, in New Zealand and overseas.

Protecting children

In his thoughtful analysis of how children have been protected over time, Ferguson (2004) ponders the following paradox: why are we consumed by anxiety over child homicide risk when, historically speaking, it has never been less risky for children than now? Contemporary systems of identification and response in child welfare are more sophisticated than ever before.

> The upshot of [this] is a greatly increased sense of risk and danger in child protection, although the actual numbers or proportion of cases involving life-threatening situations for children is small. (Ferguson, 2004, p. 116)

Risk-consciousness, according to Ferguson, has turned into risk anxiety, and social workers carry the burden of this.

To understand this phenomenon it is useful to consider what has happened over time as child homicide has gained greater public exposure. There have always been a small proportion of children who have died at the hand of adults, and the number of child deaths has remained relatively stable over recent times. But the degree of public awareness of the incidence of child homicide has varied. In the UK, child deaths known to the National Society for the Prevention of Cruelty to Children (NSPCC) were publicly reported from 1915 until 1936 (Ferguson, 2004). Subsequent known child homicides disappeared from public view, partly because of changes in the management of information, partly to allay public fears, and partly because of the fact that the number being killed had dropped to the point of being of limited significance to child welfare and child protection practice. Over time, according to Ferguson (2004, p. 90),

> [D]eath went out of sight in order to promote public trust and feelings of security in child protection and to repress people's worst social fears about families and violence.

By the mid-1970s, however, child protection work had become more visible to the general public. Awareness of child abuse was growing and increased media attention on the sexual abuse of children thrust child protection work into the limelight. The public was no longer protected paternalistically from the horrors of extreme child abuse, and the media relentlessly pursued every opportunity to bring tragic stories to public attention. Inquiries that followed these deaths began to open up systems of child welfare to public scrutiny, as Ferguson (2004, p. 110) notes:

> With the invariably aggressive attentions of the media, public disclosures of child deaths and inquiries into system 'failures' have played a crucial symbolic role in opening out child abuse and protection services, as well as professional anxiety, to public view. ... They were also shocking in the sense that they appeared to be completely new and to reflect a real decline in professional standards.

Child homicides were not new either, but they seemed new. A system of child welfare that had sought to protect the public from anxiety over child homicides now found itself being perceived as the inadequate protector of the nation's children. The impossible notion that social workers could, and should, protect all children from harm began to take root.

Public inquiries into child homicide and the rise of a culture of blame

Internationally there have been many child death inquiries over the past 30 years and much international analysis has gone into the search for practice patterns that may have been associated with these deaths (Reder et al., 1993). Child-death reviews have variously identified ways in which more co-ordinated responses can strengthen practice and support workers to do what they want to do most: protect children. In recent years, however, writers have begun to question whether these reviews, and the 'reforms' flowing from them, are actually contributing in the positive way they were originally intended:

> [They] are a clumsy and expensive way of tackling them [child homicides]. Repetitive, high-profile reviews can be counter-productive in other ways. They can reduce morale in protection agencies and drive them into unhelpfully defensive practices. They can repeatedly raise public expectations that will inevitably be disappointed, leading to scepticism and loss of support for efforts to deal with the essential problem of ill-treatment of children. (Hassall, 2006)

According to Munro (2005, p. 378), such inquiries have the potential to satisfy a community need to find a scapegoat and to 'meet that need by focusing primarily on whether any professional was at fault'. Those professionals 'bear the guilt for the disaster and ... be[come] the target of feelings of rage and frustration'. She goes on to explain that there are three mechanisms used by society and the state to minimise and/or control erratic professional behaviour:

- Punish the culprits and so encourage the others to be more diligent.
- Reduce the role of individual human reasoning as much as possible, formalising where possible with increasingly precise instructions to the human operators.
- Increase the monitoring of practice to ensure compliance with instructions. (Munro, 2005, p. 378)

For child protection social workers these three mechanisms will sound uncomfortably familiar. In terms of the first, practitioners are left in no doubt who will be blamed when a child dies. Even though professional judgements based on limited information are necessarily equivocal, they seem reasonable at the time. With the benefit of hindsight, additional information, and a high level of scrutiny, the 'right' practice pathway invariably becomes much more obvious. This is not to say that all practice decisions made by child protection social workers can be justified on the basis that professional judgement was being exercised – the issue is whether the judgement was reasonable in the circumstances given what the worker knew.

The second mechanism is used to its utmost to create practice infallibility. In trying to replace professional judgement with protocols, tools, and guidelines, it ignores the reality of the complex and changing nature of child protection work. Relying on management checklists to guide practice inhibits the development of practice frameworks that encourage deeper understandings of human motivation and reflective responses in partnership with families. Attempting to make complex matters relating to professional judgement simple by developing tools and protocols is a naïve strategy that is more likely than not to fail.

The third mechanism captures the notion of the public sector as an 'audit society' (Power, 1997). While public accountability is clearly important as it offers a means through which services can be improved, statutory social work has become subject to repeated rationalisations and reshaping within a managerial culture that seems to regard social work practice judgements as either irrational or pre-rational (Hough, 1996). This makes it much more difficult for social workers to assert the benefits of reflection, professional judgement and supervision over prescription, protocols and measurement.

Munro (2005) ponders the lack of success of these mechanisms. She notes that while the number of child deaths has not been reduced, services in the UK and US have become increasingly 'crisis-reactive' in response to abuse allegations, concentrating resources at the front end of the response system. This has meant fewer resources dedicated to early intervention and the needs of children who are at serious risk.

Risk-averse responses and the protection of children

In New Zealand, high-profile child-death reporting is one of a set of drivers that has forced our child protection system into adopting more strongly risk-averse responses in recent years. Perhaps most closely linked to the high-profile reviews is the media response to them, which usually involves a high level of media attention on child abuse and, as a consequence, strong political and community reactions. Research focusing on media attention and the number of child protection notifications received by Child, Youth and Family reveals a close correlation between the two (Mansell, 2006). High levels of media attention correspond with periods of surges in notification rates. Unsurprisingly, periods of extreme growth in notification rates follow the most intensive periods of media attention. Counter-intuitively, it does not seem to matter that the media is usually highly critical of what it believes to be poor child protection practice – notifications still flood in.

In general, notifications to Child, Youth and Family Services continue to rise steadily even in absence of high-profile cases (see Figure 4.1). This steady upward trend in notifications does not

Figure 4.1: Number of Child, Youth and Family notifications, 2000 to 2006

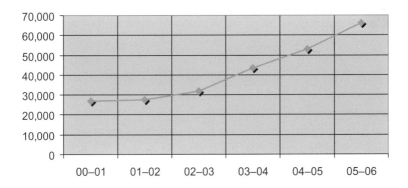

Data from The True Measure of our Success – Six Years of Achievement, *CYF & MSD, 2006, p. 15.*

necessarily reflect increasing levels of actual child abuse and neglect. More likely it reflects changes in the willingness of the public and professionals to report parental behaviour that is of concern, and also a lack of services that would better suit the needs of the children or families. New Zealand writers have also argued that this unrelenting increase in the notifications received each year is largely the result of steadily decreasing community tolerance with respect to any kind of child abuse, and a consequential rising community demand for greater state intervention to ensure the safety of children (Mansell, 2006).

Over the past 15 years, escalating community expectations that social workers must protect all children and never miss a single case of abuse have driven practice towards increasingly forensic (evidence gathering) investigations of any allegation of abuse or concern. In the context of the history of child protection practice in New Zealand this represents a disturbing shift in emphasis over time. Traditionally, practice in this country has emulated international jurisdictions, closely following practice in the UK. In the 1960s and 1970s New Zealand built an infrastructure of alternative care – foster and residential care – to provide for the needs of children who could not be cared for at home. The Children and Young Persons Act of 1974 generally supported a benign 'child rescue' model of practice. And indeed, social workers did rescue children in reasonably large numbers and placed them in care situations often for long periods of time, thus imitating the general approach of other systems of child welfare in English-speaking jurisdictions.

However, in a radical shift away from this approach, New Zealand introduced legislation in 1989 that changed the way social workers responded to children and families. It was an innovative step towards greater family participation in decision-making that drew on strongly held cultural belief systems. Rather than continuing to adopt overseas models as it had in the past, New Zealand introduced a new law incorporating a family-led process of decision-making that hoped to harness the strengths of the extended family to support the best interests of the child. It was a very different way of thinking, setting the foundation for a greater family involvement in decision-making and also greater support for them to care for their own children. The 'family support' model prevailed over the earlier 'child rescue' model in the battle for how practice should be conducted. At least that is how it seemed in 1989.

As it turned out, unexpected complications emerged. The decade of the 1990s brought new pressures, which impacted on the ascendancy of different practice models. Child welfare in New Zealand again began to emulate international developments that involved an increased emphasis on risk assessment within investigation-focused systems. Intriguingly, these professionally initiated practices found a sympathetic home within the new managerialist culture, which aimed to replace practice based on professional judgement with practice that was based on the use of standardised tools, protocols and procedures. The kind of family-led practice that blossomed after the introduction of the 1989 legislation struggled to coexist with this forensic child protection orientation. Once again, New Zealand practice started to look and sound like any other system within English-speaking jurisdictions. It was also beginning to experience the same unintended consequences.

Barter (2001) maintains that the current child protection systems are ill equipped to deal with the contemporary realities that confront families and communities, and, as a consequence, many are experiencing multi-dimensional crises. Despite many families presenting with more generic (non-abuse-specific) problems, increasingly forensically driven child protection systems have drifted towards a default position in which the large majority of families coming to attention are responded to as 'high risk' and, therefore, are exposed to a full child protection investigation. This 'one-size-fits-all' mentality means that many families are subjected to high-level, intrusive child protection assessments regardless of their need.

When notifications relentlessly increase, systems become overloaded. Spreading investigative resources too thinly results in workers being less able to identify and respond to children who really are at high risk. Social workers end up doing narrowly prescribed and often repetitive statutory tasks, usually with understandably unco-operative and resentful families. In a provocative and insightful plenary address at an international conference on child abuse and neglect held in Wellington, Scott (2006, p.1) argued that child protection systems have

> become demoralised, investigation-driven bureaucracies which trawl through escalating numbers of low-income families to find a small minority of cases in which statutory intervention is necessary and justifiable, leaving enormous damage in their wake.

Responding differently to child deaths

Reviewing each child homicide and disclosing the findings in the way we have described above has unintentionally resulted in reinforcing risk-averse practices within child care and protection. When a child dies violently, New Zealand has closely followed other countries in adopting recommendations that emerge from the child death review process. But this has often been done uncritically, using a bureaucratic rather than a professionally focused approach, with the introduction of more protocols and the revision of procedures for social workers and allied professionals, as well as concurrent demands for greater compliance. This response assumes, incorrectly, that the often idiosyncratic circumstances surrounding a single child's death can necessarily be generalised across other cases within the statutory child protection system, and that the specific professional responses that might have saved that particular child will necessarily be useful if applied more widely.

Unfortunately for other children and their families, more conservative, risk-averse practice has the potential to be reinforced across the whole system. Hence the death of one child can powerfully affect the services that are provided for all children. In reality this means that there are times when social workers and other professionals are less prepared to carry the burden of managing the risks involved in supporting families because they are likely to be blamed for not protecting (i.e. removing) a child if something goes wrong later. Taking a child into the care of the state, despite the huge emotional damage this can cause, becomes the less risky option for the social worker when compared with the option of working with the family to maintain the child within the family system.

The question that we need to ask is: what function does a practice review serve after a child has been killed? If its function, as Munro suggests, is 'to find and punish the culprit', then it may do so, but it is also likely to feed the very fears that encourage the risk-averse practices that disadvantage the majority of children who are notified to protective services. If its function is to better understand what happened in relation to a particular child homicide so that incremental improvements to systems can be made, then child death reviews that occur in a climate that supports a desire to improve services will have more positive impact. In this environment these issues can be explored and lessons learned. However, if critics selectively identify the most sensational aspects of a case out of context and reinforce a culture of blame, improvement to services is unlikely to happen.

Reviewing child deaths

A review can make no assumptions about the circumstances surrounding the death of a child. Nor can it make the assumption that the involvement of child protection services necessarily guarantees child safety. The circumstances will always be much more complex than that. What a review can do is examine the dimensions of a case and seek to understand the ways in which factors influence each other as practice decisions unfold.

A systems framework can help us explore the complex and multi-faceted aspects of casework in these tragic situations. Thinking systemically has the capacity to create a broader analysis across a set of dimensions that impact on child protection casework practice with a family. A systems analysis recognises that issues relating to child safety may be located in one or several contexts. From this beginning, a systems analysis extends the examination across a set of related dimensions – the family system, the worker system, the organisational system, and the wider system (see Figure 4.2).

Figure 4.2: A systems framework for reviewing child deaths

The family system	The worker system
The organisational system	The wider system

Exploring the family system

Ultimately the responsibility for the homicidal death of a child rests with the person who took that life. Many family factors may have contributed to the death of the child, factors that often persist regardless of professional involvement. A child death review, therefore, needs to carefully examine family characteristics that may have contributed to a child being unsafe within their family system.

It is important to understand the boundaries of the family system: who are the family members, what is their history, and who has been involved in the care of the child? What is the nature and quality of the relationships within the family, and, in particular, the attachment relationships between the primary caregiver and child? What are the significant aspects of the family dynamics – belief systems, communication patterns, history of violence, hierarchy, minimising behaviours, secrets, receptiveness to help, and strengths? What the family brought to the situation would have critically influenced how the child protection social worker(s) responded throughout the contact period. The person undertaking the review of practice needs to understand the information, characteristics, dynamics, and history of the family, or will lack insight into the professional responses that were made in the circumstances surrounding a particular death.

Exploring the worker system

Understanding professional responses to at-risk children and their families is also critical to a systems analysis of child death situations. Once involved in a child protection response, a worker's own belief system, experiences and views about children and risk become woven into the work. Given the value-driven nature of child abuse work, evaluating the degree to which these ideas influence professional judgement and conduct is important (Connolly, Crichton-Hill & Ward, 2006). It is critical to grasp the dynamics that developed between the worker and the various people within the family system. Do parallels exist between the family's and the worker's personal experiences, and did those parallels influence the ways in which the family was responded to? How did the worker understand what was happening within the family? How did this analysis influence the practice pathway selected and the way in which the work unfolded? Did the worker feel physically safe with this family, or did fears of potential violence limit the worker's ability to confront issues when necessary?

Exploring the organisational system

Practice relationships with children and their families exist within a statutory organisational context. Munro (2005) claims that this context is infused with overt and covert messages that influence the ways in which a social worker might approach working with a family. Messages about where to focus professional effort, such as ensuring compliance, can result in a worker having to choose, for example, between seeing a child or completing paperwork. As Munro (2005, p. 389) notes, 'this creates dilemmas about which matters most – the child or the performance indicator'. Compromising quality for quantity critically impacts upon the worker's capacity to engage with and understand the family and the complex safety issues related to the child.

Relevant organisational system factors also include collegial responses and the social work team context, the provision of quality supervision and the training and supports needed to foster in-depth quality practice. How has the organisation supported quality practice with this family? What opportunities have there been to reflect on and think through complex practice decisions? Have organisational processes helped or hindered the work?

Exploring the wider system

Finally, a systemic practice review cannot ignore the influence of the 'wider system'. This includes professional, community and political pressures that influence, whether overtly or covertly, social work decision-making. Exploring the wider system involves understanding the connections between the worker, the family, and the network of people and systems that surround the child. This might include other professionals, for example medical or legal systems of response.

Professional input can powerfully influence interventions with children and families. Professional hierarchies can also distort the way in which a social worker, for example, approaches a particular investigation. A practice review would need to understand how professional knowledge has influenced practice decision-making and the management of a particular situation. Has there been an uncritical reliance on external professional opinion? Has this impacted on the social worker's capacity to exercise their own professional judgement? Has a professional hierarchy undermined good practice? Have professionals worked together to provide consistency in responses, and have professional systems been sufficiently integrated to strengthen the safety net around the child?

It would seem timely to reassess the way in which we undertake child death reviews, so that we shift from reviews functioning as unintended reinforcers of risk-averse practice to ensuring that they more usefully inform practice responses. A systemic approach to reviewing a child's death from homicide entails a change of focus from minutely scrutinising the conduct of an individual social worker to considering the more complex factors and inter-relationships that invariably surround a child at risk. Child death reviews, regardless of their focus, can be used to improve services or they can be misused to search for a scapegoat. In recent years the focus on social worker error and calls for accountability and system reform have undermined the credibility and work of statutory child protection systems. This has also had the effect of weakening services and creating defensive practices that do little to support at-risk children and their families.

Rethinking our responses to child homicide has the potential to increase our understanding of the dynamics that place children at risk and to foster a culture of service improvement. We believe that using a systems framework that places practice within a wider context as the basis for child death reviews is more likely to contribute positively to the strengthening of services for children overall.

Chapter 5

Child homicide and statutory child protection services

The second half of this book focuses on managing the risk associated with child homicide within the context of systems of child welfare. In Chapter 4 we looked at child death reviews and the influence these have had on the development of risk-averse responses to child abuse notifications. In this chapter we describe the legal framework involved and the statutory system that is charged with the responsibility of protecting children, looking particularly at the professional judgements that have to be made at each stage of the process. This is an aid towards making sense of the case studies examined in Chapter 6, of a small group of children who were known to statutory child protection services prior to their deaths.

Child homicide represents the most extreme form of child abuse and, in common with most other countries, New Zealand law enables public and professional reporting of child abuse to statutory services. The approach taken in this country seeks to inform, encourage and persuade people to recognise the signs and symptoms of ill treatment and to report their concerns, ensuring legal protection for all who do so in good faith. This approach contrasts with mandatory reporting requirements in the US and in most states of Australia, but is similar to the process followed in the UK.

The adoption of mandatory reporting in New Zealand has been advocated and twice debated by Parliament. The first occasion was in 1989 during the passage of our principal child protection legislation, the Children, Young Persons and Their Families Act. The second debate occurred in 1994 when an amendment proposing mandatory reporting was withdrawn following select committee advice that a public information and awareness approach, along with a professional and occupational groups education and protocols approach were likely to be more productive and a better use of scarce resources.

Responsibilities for child protection

Within New Zealand legislation, statutory power and discretions with respect to child safety are vested in a number of individuals: the Chief Executive of the Ministry of Social Development[9]; social work staff employed by the Chief Executive; and the New Zealand Police. This contrasts with the UK, for example, where the Children Act 1989 vests statutory authority with local authorities, which in turn delegate their responsibilities to professional staff. This means that corporate bodies, not individuals, are accountable for the proper exercise of powers and functions. The fact that powers and discretions are vested in individuals is an important aspect of the legal framework in New Zealand. As a consequence, the department may provide workers with guidance in the exercise of their statutory functions, and although the department should ensure they are trained and competent to exercise their powers and discretions, it cannot dictate how these are exercised overall. The specific powers vested in the Chief Executive are usually delegated to professional staff, and, in these instances, the Chief Executive is expected to direct how these powers and authorities are to be applied.

The duty of receiving and responding to reports of child maltreatment lies with either a social worker appointed by the Chief Executive of the Ministry or with a member of the New Zealand Police. By convention, police normally refer the reports they receive to a social worker in the first instance. When a case of abuse, neglect, or insecurity of care is reported, a social worker assesses the situation and, if it is considered necessary, an investigation is undertaken. Police, health, and education agencies are frequently involved in investigations and a high degree of co-ordination is required across the spectrum of services.

Statutory officials – social workers and police – have powers to take emergency action to protect children, to arrange medical examinations, and to gather information relevant to their enquiries. New Zealand law also requires that social work professionals consult with a Care and Protection Resource Panel throughout the process of their work. These panels, which bring together individuals with a range of knowledge and skills, are statutory bodies established to provide advice to professionals as they undertake their statutory child protection duties.

Responding to suspicions of child abuse

Internationally, statutory child protection or child welfare systems vary in how they respond to notifications of child abuse or neglect. While most systems receive notifications of suspected child abuse locally, in recent years some systems have adopted a centralised system to help the initial management of abuse notifications. Since 2000, the New Zealand system of child welfare has maintained a national call-centre through which notifications to Child, Youth and Family are routed for consideration by specially trained social workers. Typically, concerns about children are received by telephone or fax and the call-centre social worker, using a set of guidelines, assesses the type of response required. On the basis of this assessment a decision is made as to whether the notification meets the threshold for a statutory investigation. This generates a number of initial response issues. On the one hand it is important that a family not be subjected to unnecessary investigation. Investigations are intrusive and can have a destabilising effect on a family. It is important therefore for the worker not to overestimate the risk for a child and so inappropriately err on the side of caution. On the other hand, underestimating risk can also have serious consequences, as shown in Figure 5.1.

Figure 5.1: Possible responses following a notification of potential abuse

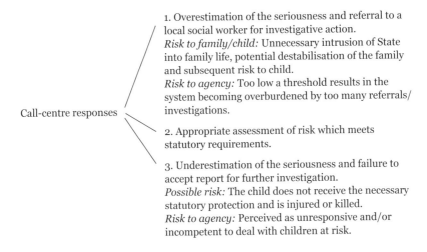

Call-centre responses

1. Overestimation of the seriousness and referral to a local social worker for investigative action.
Risk to family/child: Unnecessary intrusion of State into family life, potential destabilisation of the family and subsequent risk to child.
Risk to agency: Too low a threshold results in the system becoming overburdened by too many referrals/investigations.

2. Appropriate assessment of risk which meets statutory requirements.

3. Underestimation of the seriousness and failure to accept report for further investigation.
Possible risk: The child does not receive the necessary statutory protection and is injured or killed.
Risk to agency: Perceived as unresponsive and/or incompetent to deal with children at risk.

In the event of a report being accepted for further follow-up, a measure of criticality is also applied. This establishes a level of response urgency. The child may be assessed as being in significant danger, and under these circumstances the recommended response will be immediate. However, while assessed as being 'at risk', the child may have protectors (for example, a grandparent), or the child may be under interim protection within a safe placement. These circumstances moderate the risk, and the response urgency measure applied is likely to reflect this assessment.

A call-centre decision that a notification requires further enquiry by a statutory social worker launches a process of investigation that is guided by the recently developed care and protection practice framework (Connolly, 2006). The framework covers the three phases of the child care and protection process: engagement and assessment, seeking solutions with the family, and securing safety and belonging for the child.

Engagement and assessment

In effect the first phase of the work, engagement and assessment, involves a child protection inquiry or investigation that is undertaken by a statutory social worker. Serious allegations of sexual or physical abuse, where perpetrator identification is likely to lead to a criminal justice response, more typically involve collaboration between police and a social worker, who together plan an investigation and collect evidence under the provisions of what is known as the CYFS/Police Serious Abuse Team (SAT) Protocol.[10] This joint process is aimed at limiting the exposure of children to investigative activity. It avoids interviewing children multiple times and can satisfy the evidential requirements for both civil and criminal purposes.

The majority of child physical abuse notifications, however, are responded to directly by the social worker. Once a referral is received, statutory social workers have the power to secure a child's safety if necessary. This requires a careful consideration of the care and protection needs of the child within the context of supporting the family. Again, intervention within this phase raises a number of response issues. Undue application of statutory power may result in a child being inappropriately or prematurely removed from the family and subjected to care disruption, which can interfere with familial attachment bonds. Taking children into alternative care can injure future life chances by subjecting the child to potential placement changes, cultural dislocation, and familial disconnection. This needs to be balanced against the risk of possible further abuse, as Figure 5.2 shows.

Of course, child protection work is a complex endeavour and practice rarely falls straightforwardly within one or other of these response categories. More typically, social workers respond flexibly as the situation progresses and an intervention pathway is established. The intervention focus may shift, in either direction, as further information is gathered about the child's situation.

Research indicates that the investigative response can be hampered in situations of organisational risk: for example, when a

Figure 5.2: Potential investigative responses following abuse referral

Investigative

responses

1. Risk overestimation. Overestimation of the immediate risk to the child results in use of extreme statutory power and the child is removed from the care of family inappropriately or prematurely.
Possible risk: The child is alienated from family, attachment bonds are unnecessarily broken, and the child is subjected to an uncertain care future and longer-term damage. Engagement with the family is lost as is also the potential for enhancing longer-term safety and security outcomes for the child within the family system.

2. Appropriate risk estimation. Response reflects a balancing of child protection and family support needs. Risk of longer-term harm to the child is balanced against risk of further abuse. The situation is responded to according to departmental policy and an appropriate action plan is developed.
Possible risk: Notwithstanding the quality of the risk assessment, violence towards children can be unpredictable and family support interventions cannot, therefore, guarantee safety.

3. Indecision and delay. Response lacks decisive child protection action. Delays in allocation may occur because of resource limitations. Practice 'grey areas' or inadequate information may inhibit the social worker's capacity to move the case forward.
Possible risk: The investigation drifts, creating greater risk of the family being destabilised and/or the child remaining unprotected. The situation may change without reassessment.

4. Risk underestimation. This could involve: not sighting the child within reasonable time frame; underestimating the need for an identified protector; relying unduly on earlier assessments; unshared or unaccessed critical information; paying too little attention to the vulnerability of the very young child; not following procedures appropriately.
Possible risk: The child may not get the protective action needed to secure safety and/or the family does not get the support it needs.

system is subjected to repeated reorganisation and restructuring; when workers feel unsupported, isolated or confused about their role; or when there is inadequate servicing cover in place, such as at weekends or holiday periods (Reder et al., 1993). Research also suggests that the investigation and assessment of a report of child abuse can be a time of heightened risk for the child or children concerned. The information gathering and analysis by social workers can be affected by a number of professional stumbling blocks: the overriding belief systems held by workers; the tendency to treat information in ways that prevent pattern perception; and workers' fear of making a commitment to action (Reder et al., 1993).

The question of the level of intervention that is appropriate to the circumstances of a case has been identified as a key issue in child protection work. Practising in the face of persistent intimidation by family members or threats can impact on a social worker's ability to use his or her professional judgement to support the safety interest of the child, a situation that Goddard (1998) describes as 'accommodation syndrome'[11]. Along similar lines, Dingwell (1989, p. 163) refers to 'the rule of optimism' which, he argues, interferes not only with appropriate assessment but also decision-making in terms of whether or not an intervention is necessary. This concept involves the notion that workers gradually accept lower standards of care, a desensitisation process with effects not too dissimilar to those of the accommodation syndrome described by Goddard. That said, it is important to note that much of the research supporting these ideas was undertaken more than a decade ago. Child protection practice environments have changed considerably in the intervening period. Indeed, it could be argued that the threshold for statutory intervention has been steadily lowered in recent years to the point where more risk-averse practice is considered normative (Scott, 2006).

Regardless of what influences the assessment process, when intervention is deemed necessary the next stage of the process involves making a decision as to the form it should take.

Seeking solutions with the family

The second phase of the child protection process involves seeking solutions once concerns have been identified. Following the engagement and assessment phase of the child protection process, when the child is believed to be in need of protection the social worker is required by law to refer the child to a Care and Protection Co-ordinator who will then arrange for a Family Group Conference (FGC) to be convened. An FGC is a solution-focused meeting that brings together the child, their extended family and professionals to make decisions and develop a plan that will secure the child's care and safety. The law requires that the family be provided with private time to formulate these decisions and plans, which are then agreed to by all members of the conference. The majority of FGCs reach agreement. However, when agreement is not possible the social worker generally places the matter before the family court for resolution.

In instances where the provision of support services will adequately address the concerns, less formal interventions may be possible. A service provision agreement (Family/Whānau Agreement) may be entered into that provides support for the family, or workers may encourage families to use another legal option, such as accessing private family law provisions through the Family Court, to address their concerns. No studies have been undertaken to ascertain the effectiveness of these alternative types of intervention as a means of resolving lower-level care or protection concerns in New Zealand. However, a small qualitative study of five deaths resulting from non-accidental injury found that two deaths occurred in the investigatory phase, one while a child was subject to a Family/Whānau Agreement, and two occurred after the agency had ceased involvement with the children and families. None of these cases had been referred for a Family Group Conference (Kinley & Doolan, 1997). This issue will be further discussed in Chapter 6.

The seeking solutions with the family phase of the work also presents practice issues that may impact on the care and safety needs of the child. New Zealand practice strongly supports the development of family-led solutions for children who are considered to be at risk. Indeed, New Zealand law requires social workers to use minimally disruptive interventions in ways that strengthen family cohesiveness and connectedness. This includes respecting the capacity of family members to resolve the issues themselves, and in this regard the use of private legal options would provide a degree of independence from the child welfare system, and may well be highly appropriate in relation to the needs of the family. Nevertheless, such options may fall short of the kind of child safety monitoring required in some family situations. Service-provision agreements can provide the kind of support parents need to resolve child protection issues, but they may not have the effect of harnessing the potential contribution of the extended family and the additional support and monitoring that the extended family can provide through the mechanism of the FGC. Each of the three solutions brings with it its own set of benefits and risks as Figure 5.3 shows.

In essence, finding the best solution for a child becomes a matter of judgement for the family and the worker. A solution that works well in one family may fail to secure child safety in another. There is, however,

Figure 5.3: 'Finding solutions' options following a child protection investigation

'Finding solutions' options

1. Alternative legal options. Capturing the family in the child welfare net may not provide for the particular needs of the family, and may represent an excessive and/or unnecessary service response. Alternative legal options may be more appropriate to the family's needs and may foster a greater sense of family care and responsibility.
Possible risk: the solution does not provide adequately for the safety needs of the child.

2. Service provision agreement (Family/Whānau Agreement). This may provide a less intrusive level of support for parents to enable them to protect and care for the child.
Possible risk: the child may be isolated within the nuclear family context and may not benefit from the additional support and monitoring provided by an extended family effort.

3. Family Group Conference. This provides parents with extended family support and also ensures a greater number of adults are involved in care and safety monitoring.
Possible risks: poor FGC planning fails to harness the full strength of the extended family; insufficient or poorly organised information is presented at the FGC compromising sound decision-making; family disharmony or intimidatory family dynamics compromise sound decision-making; FGC plans are not reviewed within expected time frames.

some evidence that the family group conference approach provides safety for the child. In a UK study of 80 family group conferences, Crow and Marsh (1997) found a very low child re-abuse rate (6%) for families that had been through a family group conference, as compared to re-abuse rates (16–25%) in families that were subject to conventional child protection processes. In the same study social workers assessed that in two-thirds of their cases family group conference plans provided better protection for children than plans developed through conventional processes, and that in the other third the outcome was equal to what would have achieved using conventional processes. No case involving a family group conference was assessed as providing worse protection than would have been available through orthodox procedures. Another study (Lupton & Stevens, 1997) reported that a large majority of professionals (78%) thought FGC plans were successful. In the New Zealand context, Worrall (2001) reports that in relation to their safety there are benefits to children whose care is under the scrutiny of extended family members.

Family Group Conferences are the means of building social and familial networks that support families to provide safe environments for their children. From the international literature, social network intervention evaluations show promising and encouraging results, but controlled studies are made difficult by family mobility and dropout rates (MacDonald, 2002). In a meta-analysis of studies about what works in family-support services, it was found that working with family and social networks contributed significantly to the effectiveness of family support services (40%). It also found that the quality of the relationship between worker and family was important to good outcomes for children (30%), as was client hopefulness (15%), and the nature of the helping technique (15%) (McKeown, 2000). An analysis of 20 research projects initiated in the UK following the implementation of the Children Act 1989 concluded that children were better protected by strengthening their family and social network supports than by spasmodic, incident-focused interventions (Department of Health, 1995). By strengthening the family and social networks, we can also secure the safety of children and increase their sense of belonging.

Securing safety and belonging

The third and final phase of the child protection process described by the New Zealand practice framework is securing safety and belonging for children. This may involve supporting the child within the context of family care, or may involve placement with alternative caregivers – either kin or foster caregivers. As noted earlier, New Zealand law reinforces the importance of retaining children within the context of their family system, and in practice all social work effort should support this aim. In general, this is because the family is better able to provide for a child's longer-term needs both with respect to stability and the child's sense of identity and belonging. Inevitably, however, this produces tensions as social workers weigh up both the immediate and longer-term risks associated with keeping the child within the family as opposed to placement elsewhere.

An important aspect of the New Zealand legal framework is the support given to the primacy of family responsibility with respect to the development of plans for the child's future. Social workers are expected to support the plans developed by the family unless they seriously compromise the safety needs of the child. What constitutes 'serious' is a matter of professional judgement and in practice it is evaluated in the context of what is considered most beneficial for the child in the longer term. Again placement solutions bring their own set of benefits and risks, as shown in Figure 5.4.

These critical decisions require careful reflection and acute practice judgements that attempt to negotiate the best interests of the child in the context of both short and longer-term benefits and risks.

Many writers have noted the increasingly complex nature of contemporary child protection practice (Birmingham, Berry & Bussey, 1996; Briar-Lawson, Schmid & Harris, 1997). Fortunately, deaths of children known to statutory services are relatively rare occurrences. Nevertheless, when they do occur they can be devastating for everyone involved. Despite the rarity of these tragic deaths, anxiety about the potential for child homicide to occur strongly influences the services that are provided for at-risk children. As we noted in Chapter 4, a

Figure 5.4: Longer-term intervention options for children at risk

'Securing safety and belonging' options

1. Foster care. The placement of a child within systems of non-family care may seem to represent the safest option with respect to child homicide risk. In fact it may not necessarily provide safety and is unlikely to provide for the child's longer-term security needs.

Possible risks: alienation of the child from family support and cultural systems; child experiences drift in care and/or multiple placements that are damaging to well-being; placements may not be adequately vetted and/or there may be a shortage of adequate caregiver placements.

2. Kin care. Kinship placements may provide longer-term safety and security for the child and such placements are strongly supported by the New Zealand legal framework. Nevertheless, placements may not provide the 'ideal parenting' environments when compared with non-family caregiver arrangements, and the social worker may not be prepared to tolerate a less-than-ideal placement environment.

Possible risks: caregiver support is inadequate; family alliances undermine the child's safety needs; placement is not adequately vetted or monitored.

3. Staying at home. Supporting parents to safely care for their children is likely to represent the ideal option for children, and it is also strongly supported in New Zealand law.

Possible risk: parents are unable to provide the minimum necessary to secure the safety of the child in the longer term; support services cannot be maintained; child is subjected to multiple care systems and re-notifications.

child protection system that is both risk-averse and defensive is likely to result in increasing numbers of children moving into care. Such a system is clearly not risk-free for children (Berridge & Cleaver, 1987; Department of Health and Social Security [DHSS], 1985; Packman, Randall & Jacques, 1986; Triseliotis, 1989).

Managing ambiguity and informed risk-taking are key components of child care and protection social work. In the early 1990s, new child welfare law in New Zealand called for more flexible and innovative approaches to resolving problems within at-risk families. Changes in the law granted workers greater autonomy and authority to negotiate options and seek common ground with family networks. Unfortunately for care and protection practices in this country, by the end of that decade services had become more restricted, conservative and procedure-bound as a result of a complex interplay of political, organisational and professional pressures.

It is to this decade of the 1990s that we now turn to examine case studies of children who died as a result of homicide and who were known to statutory child protection services prior to their deaths.

Notes

[9] The operational functions are provided through Child, Youth and Family, a service of the Ministry of Social Development.

[10] This is an inter-agency protocol that guides investigations of sexual or serious physical abuse.

[11] Goddard proposes that faced with overwhelming threat and intimidation by a frightening, controlling family member, workers can, over time, begin to accommodate behaviour that in any other circumstance they would find unacceptable. In effect, workers are taken hostage and their focus shifts from protecting the child to appeasing the aggressor.

Chapter 6
The deaths of children known to statutory services

In Chapters 2 and 3 we examined the scope and nature of child homicide in a broad international and national context. We now move on to a more detailed qualitative analysis of a small subset of the 91 cases we looked at in Chapter 3. The subset is comprised of nine children who died from non-accidental injuries in the five years from 1996 to 2000 and were known to statutory child protection services in New Zealand. A closer examination of the children who died prior to 1995 has not been possible because national records were not kept at that time. As the group of children whose information is available is very small, statistical analysis is neither possible nor appropriate. Instead, qualitative case analysis of information provided by Child, Youth and Family will be used to illuminate the issues associated with assessment and intervention. Qualitative analysis of written records provides a rich source of information from which more subtle interpretations can be drawn (Liamputtong & Ezzy, 2005). This adds further richness to the insights gained from the analysis of the data recorded by the police over the same period.

While the quantitative analysis discussed in Chapter 3 has been useful in describing the phenomenon of child homicide in New Zealand, it has, by the very nature of the available data, been focused on the child and the perpetrator. The qualitative component of the study described in this chapter enables a greater level of analysis in terms of the complex interplay between family, community, professionals, and organisational systems that is the background in these tragic outcomes for children. In addition, identifying the professional complexities surrounding the circumstances of each child's death has the capacity to inform professional and organisational systems in terms of further developing their responsiveness to children at risk.

There is a widely held assumption that the children who die as a result of homicide will have been known to statutory child protection services. However, in our study we found that only 19% of all child homicide cases in the period 1996–2000 involved children who were known to the department. As noted in Chapter 2, this can be compared with international findings where studies in the US, Australia and the UK have found the proportion of cases with prior agency contact ranged from 25% to almost 80%. The New Zealand data summarised in Table 6.1 is drawn from unpublished police and child welfare records. Two of the deaths recorded by Child, Youth and Family[12] were not recorded in the police statistics.

It is difficult to gauge how New Zealand's 'known to agency' rate of 1 in 5 lines up with experiences elsewhere, given the issues of

Table 6.1: Homicides of children 14 years and under and numbers of these known to CYF prior to the death of the child, 1996–2000

Year	All deaths	Known to CYF	Percentage known to CYF
1996	5[13]	0	0
1997	13	2	15
1998	8	3	37
1999	12	3	25
2000	9	1	11
Total	**47**	**9**	**19**

counting and definitional imprecision, whether or not studies took a broad or narrow view of what constitutes a child protection agency, and the time frames in which the data were collected. One source (Pecora et al., 1992) claims a substantial number of the families in which these tragedies occurred had been reported to, or served by child protection services, and there are estimates that as many as 80% of the families will have come to notice. However, an Australian estimate of 1 in 4 such families having prior contact with child protection authorities (Armytage & Reeves, 1992) provides some reassurance that the finding of this study is not markedly different. Another significant point is that within the New Zealand national statistics, almost a quarter of the children who died were involved in multiple homicide incidents. As noted in Chapter 3, we really know very little about the circumstances surrounding the deaths of these children, but if they do represent cataclysmic family events in the context of a parental dispute then they may not be cases that have a history of child abuse and therefore would not have come to the attention of Child, Youth and Family. We also do not know how many single deaths may have occurred within this context.

Characteristics of the children

The nine children in this qualitative study were aged from 8 months to 12 years: six were under 5 years of age, including two under 1 year, and three were over 5 years. Six were Māori and three Pākehā. Five were boys and four were girls. None of the children died as a result of acts of omission, but rather all were killed by violent actions – five were battered, three stabbed, and one was suffocated.

Characteristics of the perpetrators

There were ten perpetrators: seven men, including three who were biological fathers, and three women, including two who were biological mothers and one who was the partner of one of the mothers. Five were de facto parents.[14] Thus all the deaths qualify as cases of intra-familial homicide. Five of the nine cases were filicide, three perpetrated by the father, one by the mother, and the fifth by a mother acting jointly with her female de facto partner (hence the count of 10 perpetrators for 9 child deaths). The other four deaths occurred at the hands of the parent's male de facto partner.

In none of these families did the child's biological parents cohabit. In four cases the child's custodial parent had undergone a partnership change (in one case the resumption of a former relationship) in the months before the child's death, and in three of these cases the new partner was the perpetrator. Two further cases involved de facto relationships where the length of the relationship was unable to be discerned from case data. Three cases involved sole parents.

Contact with child protection services

The records held by Child, Youth and Family provide information about the circumstances of each child prior to their death. Information relating to the number of notifications[15] received for each child, the reasons for each notification, and the person who made the notification are set out in Table 6.2.

Reports to Child, Youth and Family

Child, Youth and Family received a total of 16 reports in the form of referrals or notifications about the nine children prior to their deaths. In one case three reports were received, in five cases two, and in three cases only one report was received before death occurred. Concerns about abuse, neglect, welfare, and care arrangements dominated these reports. Physical abuse was cited in four of the nine cases.

The dilemma for any child care and protection agency is how to rate the urgency of notifications alleging neglect or expressing concerns about a child's environment alongside those of outright physical abuse. Understandably, there will be a tendency to respond first to overtly physical abuse episodes. However, the fact that a number of the children were reported for concerns other than physical abuse but

Table 6.2: Details of the nine children known to Child, Youth and Family

Child	Referral/ Notification	Reason for CYF involvement	Referrer/ Notifier	Perpetrator of child homicide	Date of death	Age at death
A F*	1st 29.11.96 2nd 11.03.97	Neglect Court-ordered custody/access report	Father Court	Father	09.09.97	2 years 11 months
B F	1st 24.02.97 2nd 14.08.97 3rd 10.09.97	Sexual abuse by father Sexual abuse by father Abduction	Father's ex-partner Rape Crisis Worker School	Father	10.09.97	12 years
C M**	1st 13.08.97 19.08.97	Neglect Abuse/neglect	Agency Member of Public	De facto father	09.02.98	1 year 5 months
D M	1st 08.09.97 2nd 08	Neglect Neglect	Agency Family friend	De facto father	08.06.98	11 months
E F	13.08.98	Court-ordered custody/access report	Court	Father	16.12.98	8 years
F M	1st 19.07.96 2nd 23.01.97	Physical abuse Court-ordered custory/access report	Police Court	De facto father	05.04.99	4 years
G F	25.02.99	Welfare	School	Mother and de facto partner (female)	10.05.9	6 years
H M	1st 08.03.99 2nd 13.08.99	Physical abuse Physical abuse	Health professional Health professional	Mother	20.08.99	8 months
I M	17.12.99	Physical abuse/ neglect	Agency	De facto father	12.01.00	4 years

* Female

** Male

were subsequently physically harmed highlights the importance of considering the particular vulnerabilities of children, particularly very young children.

Staff from professional or helping agencies made the majority of the reports, with a minority made by family members. That professionals made so many of the reports about these children is some validation of efforts made to educate professionals about the signs and symptoms of abuse and of reporting pathways. It is interesting to note the lower level of family or friends' input in terms of approaches to Child, Youth and Family in cases that eventually involved a fatality.

Statutory social work process and the occurrence of homicide

An examination of the records kept by Child, Youth and Family identified a range of social work activities, including care and protection interventions for the children who died, and also Child, Youth and Family responses to requests for information required for custody or access applications. Table 6.3 locates the homicides within these social work activities.

Assessment and intervention following notification

1.   *In one case, after a notification was received, a decision was made on the basis of the worker's assessment that there was no need for service involvement and the intake was closed (no further action required).*

There was no investigation in this case. The school contacted Child, Youth and Family when the child was distressed about going home with her caregiver. Following the initial information, the social worker spoke to the child and the caregiver and the cause of the child's distress was explained as the change in arrangements for her to visit her mother. The social worker spoke again to the school and accepted assurances about the child's safety and the school's monitoring system. The case was therefore closed. There were no

Table 6.3: Incidence of child homicide across phases of CYF involvement

Phases of CYF involvement	Number of homicides
1. Intake (closed, no further action required)	1
2. Investigation and assessment	3
3. Intervention solutions: a Family/Whānau Agreement[16] b Family Group Conference Plan (or court-ordered plan following an FCG)	2 0
4. Alternative private legal arrangements (Guardianship Act 1968)[17]	3

further notifications of concern about this child, who was killed three months later.

2. *In three cases, the homicide occurred during the investigation phase.*

a. In the first of these cases, two notifications raised concerns about the mental health of a mother and the care of her small baby. Following the first notification, mental health social workers maintained a key role with respect to supporting the mother, and the Child, Youth and Family investigation was closed. Child protection social workers relied heavily on mental health professionals and lay people to provide the mother with support. A second notification was made when the child was in hospital. Four days later the case was allocated to a social worker and an investigation plan was developed. Varying information was received from medical professionals about the mother's current presentation and her care of the baby, and the social worker made arrangements to visit the day following discharge. The social worker was unable to visit as arranged and the baby died two days later. The situation highlights the importance of working collaboratively across mental health/child protection boundaries and the need to ensure that information required to inform casework decisions is clarified. In the end the conditions changed quickly and the child was left in an unsafe situation.

b. The second case relates to a four-year-old child who was killed by his mother's de facto partner. The initial notification information came from an anonymous caller. The notification was assessed as not requiring an immediate response, but was nevertheless followed up within the days just before Christmas. The social worker was unable to locate the child and his family, who were understood to have left the area for the Christmas period. A member of the child's extended family undertook to monitor the well-being of the child and his siblings until the family's return in the New Year. The child was killed early in January before further follow-up occurred.

c. The third case relates to a twelve-year-old girl who died during the investigation phase. She was killed by her father following allegations of sexual abuse by him. The father admitted to the police that he had been sexually abusing his daughter and was charged and released on bail on condition that he not associate with the child. Within two weeks of being charged with sexual abuse, the father abducted the child from school and she died that day of multiple stab wounds. In the practice review of the case, a number of general systemic issues occurring within the agency were indicated, but these were not considered to have a direct impact on the events of the case.

3.   *In two cases a Family/Whānau Agreement was recommended as the level of intervention.*

a. In the first of these cases a notification was received from a social service agency reporting concerns of neglect. The wider family members also expressed concerns about the welfare of the three children in the family. Two older children were taken into care, but the infant who subsequently died was left at home. The social worker consulted with the Care and Protection Resource Panel, convened a professionals' case conference and then organised a family meeting at which a Family/Whānau Agreement was proposed and accepted. Although there was no formal risk assessment, the risk was considered to be one of neglect and a supportive casework response was indicated. Perhaps most significantly the mother entered a new relationship, which was unknown to Child, Youth and Family, and the child died within two weeks at the hands of the mother's de facto partner. The last visit by a social worker was four weeks before the child's death. A report following the death indicated that the circumstances surrounding the death could not have been foreseen.

b. In the second case, one notification was made to Child, Youth and Family. The concern was related to the neglect and failure to thrive of two young children. The investigation was inconclusive, and when the mother and children moved to another part of the country the investigating social worker's recommendation to the new district was for a Family/Whānau Agreement, but the worker also raised the possibility of a Family Group Conference. The social worker in the new district visited once but did not sight the children. One of the children subsequently died at the hands of the mother's de facto partner. An investigation plan had been developed but had not been formally recorded in the Child, Youth and Family information system. No formal risk assessment was undertaken. A greater focus on the child's needs may have strengthened practice with respect to the family. The practice review of the case reported that there was nothing to indicate the tragedy could have been foreseen or averted.

2.   *In three cases alternative legal arrangements under the Guardianship Act 1968 were utilised.*

a. In the first of these cases the notification made to Child, Youth and Family was based on concerns about the infant's living situation. This led to the child being removed from the mother's care and placed with her natural father and his new partner. The mother had identified the father as someone who could care for the children in the longer term. The social worker supported the father's intention to seek guardianship and custody under alternative legal arrangements. No assessment of the father's parenting capacity appears to have been made. The father, however, reported significant management difficulties with the child and requested information about parenting courses and counselling, although he did not want ongoing involvement with Child, Youth and Family. The case was closed when the father was granted interim custody and assurances were obtained from a health professional that there would be regular monitoring of the situation. The child died at the hands of her father two weeks later.

b. In the second case, prior to the death the child was already subject to alternative legal care provisions. The court asked for a report from a Child, Youth and Family social worker in relation to an application from one parent, the mother, to resume custody. The parent who had custody of the child at that time, the father, had a history of a mental health disorder and there were some indications that his condition was deteriorating. However, as the father and child lived with the grandparents, this living arrangement was considered by the worker to be a protective factor. The father killed the child on the evening of the day in which the court agreed to a change of custody to the mother and before the custody transfer was possible. The practice review of the case reported that the social worker was considered to have acted professionally.

c. In the third case a pre-school-age child was killed by his mother's de facto partner, who had previously been imprisoned for an assault on the same child. At the time of the first assault, social workers encouraged the grandmother to seek custody and guardianship of the child under family law provisions. In their assessment she had the strength to prevent further contact between her daughter, as the mother of the child, and her daughter's de facto partner when he emerged from prison. The perpetrator's likely internment was expected to be less than six months. Social workers withdrew from the case because in their assessment, the child was safe. When released from prison, however, the de facto partner was ordered to live at the same address as the child's mother. A number of agencies were involved with the family. For example, in the space of two or three years, the child had had more than 40 separate contacts, many of which were injury related, with a variety of medical professionals. There appeared to be little co-ordination or exchange of information between services involved with the family. The child died two years after Child, Youth and Family had closed the case.[18]

Issues raised by the case studies

The small number of cases considered here prevents us from drawing firm conclusions from the data. They do, nevertheless, promote areas of useful discussion that help to illuminate the tensions and issues inherent in child care and protection practice.

Neglectful parenting notifications

Three of the nine children who died were referred to Child, Youth and Family with neglect as the predominant concern. In contrast, three other cases involved physical abuse as the primary concern, while in one case sexual abuse was indicated. Situations of neglect are frequently responded to by a supportive casework response (this may include home visiting by a helping professional, developing formal and informal supports, parenting education and skill development, the support of positive parent–child interactions, developing a helping alliance based on trust, and securing concrete resources when necessary). In part, the supporting casework approach is utilized because it is generally considered possible to monitor and respond to any deterioration within a family situation and to intervene if this is necessary. Given the history of the three cases where neglect was the presenting concern, and the fact that none involved previous notifications for physical abuse, the assessment of risk and subsequent decisions to provide support appears to be a reasonable service response. Nevertheless, the three children experienced violent deaths.

Although in these situations fatal events proved difficult to anticipate, the cases we examined suggest that social workers need to remain alert to the possibility that other forms of abuse may occur. Could the deaths of the three neglected children have been averted? Could the social workers have been more vigilant in terms of physical abuse risk? Would a formal risk assessment have alerted the social workers to that potential danger? As Munro (2002, p. 85) argues, 'the best guide to future behaviour is past behaviour'. The absence of a history of physical abuse means that predicting future abuse is more akin to crystal-ball gazing. Herein lies a harsh but inevitable reality in terms of child protection practice: not all violence towards children can be anticipated, nor is it appropriate to treat all families who struggle to adequately care for their children as potential child killers. What is important is that we develop systems of response that are the best that they can be, and that these systems understand the dynamics of abuse, and the ways in which abuse and neglect dynamics inter-relate.

The impact of alternative legal arrangements

In three of the cases in this study the children were involved in Family Court proceedings prior to their death. Given the tragic outcomes, it is important that we understand the circumstances surrounding these deaths.

The three cases present us with a range of different circumstances. In the last family situation (4c) the family history and level of risk indicated by previous violence raise significant questions regarding the lack of decisive child protection responses. In the space of two or three years, one child had more than 40 separate contacts with medical professionals, many of which were due to suspicious injuries. His stepfather, imprisoned for abusing him, was expected to be released in a relatively short period of time. The child's safety was reliant on the strength of a grandmother in the face of an abusive, aggressive male who had been imprisoned for a violence-related crime. It is reasonably clear that the circumstances surrounding the situation were serious and that the level of risk was high.

Statutes play different roles in ensuring the needs of a child are met. Private law options available through the Family Court are not primarily designed to secure the safety of a child. They are specifically directed toward the care of children following parental dispute. The public law provisions of the Children, Young Persons and Their Families Act 1989 enable a formal investigation process and statutory response options that are specifically designed to respond to the protection needs of a child. In the case of this very vulnerable pre-school child, this legislation would have provided a far more appropriate method of dealing with the level of risk within the family and of securing a greater level of safety for the child.

The other two cases in which alternative legal arrangements were granted are not quite so clear-cut. In the first case (4a), the father sought guardianship and custody through the Family Court. Although there appeared to have been no assessment of his care-giving capacity, there had been no previous concerns in relation to this. While it was clear that he did not want ongoing involvement with Child, Youth and Family, he had described some significant behavioural problems of his daughter and he was receptive to counselling support. Nevertheless, the degree of concern he expressed about his daughter's behaviour was such that the need for an ongoing role for Child, Youth and Family may well have been indicated.

This was a professional judgement call, based on what seemed reasonable at the time. In hindsight, once the tragic consequences are known, alternative responses can be readily identified. It is clear though that social workers need to be child-centred and focus attention on the needs of the specific child in these challenging situations and not just on the caregiver issues. There is a need to undertake robust assessments of parenting ability and capacity, particularly in the face of extreme child behavioural issues.

The second situation (4b) involved a custody dispute in which the social worker was asked to report on a parent's application to resume custody. A change of custody was decided by the court, but the child was killed by the custodial parent before the custody transfer could be made. Was the situation of sufficient concern to the social worker to have warranted independent child protection action? The custodial parent did have a mental health disorder and there was some indication that the condition was deteriorating. But such situations are not uncommon in custody disputes, and given the lack of previous abuse history, it is not clear that child protection action was warranted at the time. Importantly, the parent and child were living with the grandparents and that was seen as a protective factor for the child. Given the potential dangers for children immediately following changes in custody arrangements, this case reminds us of how important it is to carefully consider how custody decisions are implemented and whether there are additional safety concerns for the child.

In Chapter 5 we noted that almost a quarter of the 91 child homicides that occurred between 1991 and 2000 involved multiple deaths. It is not known whether these multiple homicides involved children who were the subjects of custody disputes between their parents, although some such cases have received attention in the literature – for example, one case where the father killed his three daughters and then himself (Busch & Robertson, 1994). However, we do know it is a time of risk for children and that some children do die in the context of these disputes. It is critical, therefore, that we find out more about the circumstances surrounding the deaths of such children and that this knowledge informs services that are provided in the context of decisions made in the Family Court under the provisions of the Care of Children Act 2004.

Understanding relationships within the family

In a number of the cases that we have examined, there were important issues involving the child's relationship with a caregiver. The dynamics involved in the caregiver–child relationship ultimately created dangers for the child. A number of the children were killed by a parent's de facto partner. While being step-parented is identified in the literature as a risk factor, within this small study the issue was more to do with the quality of the relationship between the caregiver and the child rather than the step-parenting relationship per se. Poor attachment bonds were apparent and the de facto partner's attitude to the child was either emotionally ambivalent, or hostile.

The quality of the relationships between biological parents and their children was also an issue reflecting complex relationship dynamics. Two of the parents had a very intense and enmeshed relationship with their child (one involved sexual abuse) and a further two had recently become the primary caregiver. Again, the quality and nature of the relationship between parent and child is critical to the understanding of potential risk.

Case allocation and the FGC

In this small study no child died during the period prior to case allocation. In recent years, considerable concern has been expressed, particularly in media reports, that children have not received the necessary child protection response within reasonable time frames. The fact that children have remained on waiting lists has generated significant concern. Levels of risk will vary from case to case with respect to unallocated children. However, in this study of nine cases at least, the management of unallocated cases was not a factor in any of the deaths.

It is of interest that during the period under study (1995–2000) no children whose families had been through a Family Group Conference were killed. These conferences can have the effect of increasing the number of potential protective agents within the child's social and familial contexts. The FGC provides the first real opportunity for the extended family to work together to resolve the problems they face. Engaging the strengths of the wider family group provides the opportunity to broaden the safety-net for the child. In addition, holding a Family Group Conference triggers a number of processes and activities, including family-led decision-making and the development of a family plan to address the issues of concern.

Additional professionals become involved in the case, for example the Care and Protection Co-ordinator who convenes the FGC, whose role is to focus on the best interests of the child. Where the Family Court is already involved (say in cases where emergency protective action has been initiated), a Counsel for the Child will have been appointed to work with other professionals and ultimately represent the best interests of the child within the court context.

The FGC process has become well known internationally, and is perceived as characterising the New Zealand approach to child care and protection. As noted in the previous chapter, there is some evidence from international research that the Family Group Conference is an effective decision-making forum, and that the utilisation of the FGC is seen by workers to be a key mechanism in providing good outcomes for children.

Having looked at the circumstances of nine children who were known to Child, Youth and Family prior to their deaths, it seems that that few of the deaths could have been anticipated. As Ferguson (2004, p. 218) insightfully notes: 'Ultimately, we even have to be prepared to face the uncomfortable fact that any guarantees in protecting children are simply beyond the capacities of what human beings are capable of, even trained professional ones'. Child protection work is complex, and despite the relentless search for professional error when a child dies, it is important to understand that interventions can fail for a variety of reasons. Families may be unco-operative and evasive in their responses to professional assessments of risk to children. Some vulnerable parents lack the capacity to form and maintain healthy relationships with their children and, indeed, have difficulty coming to trust those professionals seeking to protect them. Ultimately this may undermine the protective actions of others (Ferguson, 2004). This is not to say that accepting the unavoidable fallibility of professional systems means we give up hope. Indeed, the research and insights we have commented on in the second half of this book offer an opportunity to rethink the way we respond to incidents of child homicide, so that we can avoid the unintended consequences and build up our services to be the best that they can be to protect the interests of children. We now draw these ideas together and consider their implications in our final chapter.

Notes

[12] The department's name changed several times during the period under discussion but for convenience sake we refer to it as Child, Youth and Family throughout.

[13] One child was in the care of Child, Youth and Family because of the injury that ultimately led to death. Prior to that injury, the child had had no contact with statutory child protection services. This child has, therefore, not been included in the qualitative analysis.

[14] We define de facto parents as adults in a relationship with the biological parent, but not themselves biologically related to the child.

[15] Notifications include information formally recorded as a notification or information received in the nature of a notification.

[16] A Family/Whānau Agreement is an informal agreement that entails providing social work support and services for a family. Such an agreement was proposed in one case but the child died before it was implemented.

[17] The Guardianship Act 1968 has now been replaced by the Care of Children Act 2004

[18] The death of this child received extensive media attention and was reviewed by the Children's Commissioner. For a full discussion of the publicly available review and its recommendations see OCC (2000).

Chapter 7

Using knowledge in policy and practice

In this book we have examined factors that contribute to child homicide in New Zealand and the ways in which fatal abuse cases have been responded to by our statutory system of child welfare. We found these responses had implications for other children and their families and the agencies that support them. In this final chapter, we draw together what we consider to be the key issues from the research and our discussions, and look at the options as we build systems of response for children at risk. First, we look at what is happening for families.

What happens inside the family

As the majority of child homicides are filicide (that is, the child is killed by a biological parent), and the remainder mostly occur within the child's care-giving situation where the perpetrator is known to the child, family factors have a major impact on child deaths. There are indications in the literature that families in which serious child maltreatment occurs tend to have some common characteristics – parental youthfulness, low educational attainment, relationship instability, spousal violence, and multiple stressors impacting on adult functioning in the households.

Although many families that display various indicators of negative well-being will still be safe and nurturing environments for children (Ministry of Social Development, 2004), the presence of these indicators in families that do abuse can guide the design of helping services, and also give important impetus and direction to policy and practice interventions that support families. There is enormous potential for things to go wrong when the factors that mould families are also significant stressors in their lives. We continue, nevertheless, to lack data that would help us better understand these issues. For example, as we noted in Chapter 3, an Australian study found that just over a third of child homicide situations involved a parent killing their child before committing suicide (Lawrence, 2004). Custody disputes and conflict over child access can engender feelings of jealousy, rage and possessiveness, and these situations clearly present risks for some children. We know little about this phenomenon in New Zealand, although we note that in the time frame under study, police statistics contain what appear to be eight instances of multiple homicides by a caregiver, some of which may be linked to adult relationship breakdown and dispute between parents. Without looking into these situations in greater depth we are unable to confirm what they actually represent. Nor can we tell how many single child deaths follow couple separation or dispute. One of the cases in Child, Youth and Family's records that did involve a custody struggle between the child's natural parents indicated something of the vulnerability of younger children in these circumstances. The coincidence of homicide with custody battles being fought out in the Family Court may prove to be of more relevance than its coincidence with child care and protection issues.

The common experience of family disruption and transition in the small case sample of children known to Child, Youth and Family during the period under study raises issues with respect to the lack of intra- and extra-family support, and the particular dangers for children within these contexts. Although this area of research is underdeveloped, studies suggest that multiple transitions are associated with increased levels of risk for children (Pryor & Rodgers, 2001). Family instability may also be exacerbated by the increasing isolation of families, particularly young Māori families, from traditional collective child-rearing arrangements. In the past, intergenerational child-rearing responsibilities gave support to young parents, but also provided alternative avenues for children to receive the love and nurturance that is important to healthy development. Children rejected or poorly treated by their parents could find safe haven within the context of their extended family. While intergenerational caring occurs in Māori households to a greater degree than it does in non-Māori households (MSD, 2004), many young Māori adults with child-rearing responsibilities may be alienated from their whānau, hapū, iwi, and be without the compensatory effects of any alternative nurturing systems of support. In situations of child abuse and neglect, New Zealand's child welfare legislation provides a context within which a child's extended family can be reconnected in order to function more strongly as a protective factor within the child's life. Utilising these mechanisms is an important component of contemporary child protection practice.

Perhaps most compelling in our small qualitative study was the number of times bonding and attachment issues featured. While some of the children died at the hands of a parent's de facto partner, it was not necessarily the type of relationship per se, but rather the quality of the attachment bond between the child and the de facto parent that is cause for concern. This concern was not confined to non-biological relationships. We found that the quality of attachment and bonding was also an issue in the relationships between biological parents and their children. Many of the parent–child relationships were characterised by emotional ambivalence and/or enmeshment on the part of the parent, or were openly fraught. It is important that professionals understand the strength of the caregiver–child bond, which inevitably makes the parent more or less of a protector for the child. While changes in caregivers and/or relationships within the household need to be considered when making risk assessments, it is most important for the social worker to understand the nature and quality of the adult–child relationships and the strength of the attachment bonds, and to factor these into the assessment of risk.

Although this book has focused on child homicide, the issue of neglectful parenting is one that perhaps deserves particular mention in the context of child mortality. Fatal child neglect does not tend to be the focus of media headlines, and in general receives less research and policy attention (Lawrence & Irvine, 2004). Yet children who are neglected do feature in both child death and child homicide situations. Examining child deaths over a three-year period from 1999–2001, Australian research has attributed the deaths of 31 children to fatal neglect (Sankey, 2003). There are, however, significant difficulties in identifying fatal neglect deaths, and it is, therefore, unclear whether this figure underestimates the true number.

Although fatal neglect can occur with children of any age, infants are particularly vulnerable. This is essentially because they are more physically vulnerable and entirely dependent on adults to care for and protect them. For example, babies may struggle to survive being rolled upon when sleeping alongside an over-tired parent, or a parent in a drug- or alcohol-induced sleep. Hence, extra practice vigilance is necessary when working with infants and their families. In a very practical response to this type of death (known as 'overlaying' in the international context), the Illinois Department of Children and Family Services in the US now provides all families who present with vulnerable infants a cot/crib to discourage the parental practice of sleeping with the baby. As a result, there has been a dramatic decrease in the number of babies who die from overlaying.[19]

This is an interesting idea and one that may be worth considering within the New Zealand context. It is important, however, that any initiatives to promote safe sleeping practices also accommodate positive cultural practices. For example, a parent sleeping with a baby – not an uncommon practice with Pacific families – is also likely to produce a strong attachment bond between the parent and child. This is important, particularly given our earlier discussion relating to the quality and strength of parent–child attachments. Developing cribs that enable a child's close proximity to the parent, while at the same time promoting safe sleeping practices, is more likely to resonate with cultural practices within New Zealand. To this end, innovative work is currently being undertaken to develop a 'wahakura' (waha – carrying in a comforting way, kura – precious little object)[20]. The wahakura

(Figure 7.1) is a smallish, woven bassinet for an infant that is placed in the bed between parents. Developed as a way of addressing health risk factors in Sudden Infant Death Syndrome, it may also provide additional protections for children more generally.

When we looked into the family life of the children in our small study, we found that there were times when children were reported for neglect but were subsequently violently killed by a parent or caregiver. In these situations, when there is a lack of any previous history of abuse or violence, it would be difficult to anticipate the possibility of a violent death occurring. Nevertheless, the vulnerability of the younger child in particular, means that we need to explore ways in which they can be better protected in ambiguous situations. Because these situations often require a careful and reflective analysis of the child's situation within the context of the family, it is important that services

Figure 7.1: Wahakura

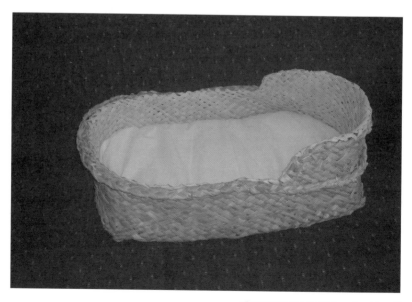

Photo provided by David Tipene Leach (2006).
Reproduced with permission.

create opportunities for workers to discuss these cases and explore the subtleties that they present in practice. Supervision and practice leadership is critical to this process, and so too is the development of resources that encourage in-depth rather than 'conveyor belt' practice (Ferguson 2004, p. 211)[21].

Practice frameworks have the capacity to provide opportunities for this kind of reflective practice (Connolly, 2006). As evidence-based resources, they can integrate knowledge about what works, and can also be used to interrogate practice by providing triggers or reminders to explore the ways in which the child and family is being responded to. In situations of neglect, practice triggers need to highlight the particular vulnerability of babies and the connections between neglectful and abusive parenting.

Our research on the police data reinforces the vulnerability of the younger child with respect to physical harm and child homicide. Rates of death from abuse are higher for children under 5 years, and are highest for children under 1 year of age. Four key elements have been identified as being important when working with this group of children (Child, Youth and Family & Ministry of Social Development, 2006). First, it is important to *target* at-risk infants by identifying them early and developing high-quality, timely responses across the spectrum of human services. Having a shared understanding of the risk factors is important in this collaborative response. Second, *building capacity* across the sector is necessary in order to respond to the diverse needs of children and families. This includes developing and sharing specialist expertise, and exploring appropriate means of sharing information. The third key element has been identified as *co-ordination* across agencies, particularly when working with vulnerable infants. In general, writers agree that co-ordinated responses result in more effective interventions (Bell, 1999; McIntosh, 2000). Despite the identified strengths of a collaborative approach, difficulties in inter-agency communication and co-ordination have plagued child welfare services over many years. Hallett and Birchall (1992, p. 26) identify a number of issues that increase the complexity of professionals working together:

> ... different professional perspectives and frames of reference
> about the nature of child abuse and of intervention, different
> agency mandates and operational priorities or organization
> tendencies towards autonomy, the time and other resource
> costs of collaborative work and interpersonal difficulties of
> trust and openness, gender and status differentials.

Overcoming these difficulties and tensions through integrated models of service provision will help to strengthen practice with vulnerable children.

The fourth element that has been identified as important when working with vulnerable babies is *monitoring and responding*. This includes developing co-ordinated review and monitoring systems for infants at risk. Because things can change quickly for babies, vigilance toward changing conditions that may increase risk and providing swift, co-ordinated responses to elevated risk are particularly important. Within the context of protective services, intensifying supervision and strengthening in-depth reflective practice, as we have described above, is critical when working with this vulnerable group.

What happens outside the family

The cases we examined in Chapter 6 illustrate the complexities of child protection practice. Practice is often fraught with anxiety, uncertainty, secrecy and/or misleading or incomplete information. It challenges adult behaviour and adult concepts of child ownership. Strong reactions and negative responses can be directed towards workers, who may need the courage and tenacity to persevere when faced with aggressive, passive, or avoidant behaviour from caregivers responsible for the welfare of children, and they have a right to strong agency support. Yet this kind of courageous practice may fail in a society that focuses on allocating blame when things go wrong, and when protection systems consequently tend towards anxiety-reducing risk aversion. In Chapter 4 we noted how media 'scandal politics' can influence public perceptions of child homicide and the services that respond to children at risk. Media and political responses are not consequence free. A sensationalist media that fosters community panic and a 'seek-the-culprit' mentality has to accept some responsibility for ultimately working against the interests of children. They promote a climate that pushes services toward legalistic and reactive systems (Scott, 2006). The louder and more vocal the 'scandal politics' get, the less able protection services will be to protect children. In this environment social workers become less prepared to work with ambiguity and take more conservative action, when managing the risk and supporting the family might better serve a child's interests. Ironically, this is all happening at a time when it has never been less risky for children:

> The paradox is that social worker's fears and anxieties have multiplied at a time when the actual phenomenon of child death in child protection is such an extremely rare experience that only a tiny fraction of professionals will ever encounter it. (Ferguson, 2004, p. 122)

More families get caught in the risk-averse child welfare net as social workers do more and more investigations in an attempt to make practice risk-free for children. The sad flaw in this unintended risk-averse approach rests in its absolute impossibility. Social work practice, as a human endeavour, can never be perfect.

It is time to call a truce. Child welfare systems need to be strong and courageous to protect the interests of children. And they need to be supported to do so. We can expect them to do only what is humanly possible. And when they fail at times, as they invariably will, we need to support them through the process so that these tragedies do not critically damage the system and its broader capacity to serve the interests of the majority of our children. For, as Ferguson (2004, p. 7) notes: 'The future safety of many children is at the same time inherently linked to the wellbeing and effectiveness of social work as the primary statutory child protection agency'. Scott (2006) suggests we may well be at a crossroads in the history and development of child protection.

Where to from here?

Child protection experts have begun to raise questions about the way in which systems respond to the death of a child by homicide (Munro, 2002; Scott, 2006). Faced with pressure to develop a 'silver bullet', organisations introduce more guidelines and tools, or adopt new ideological models aimed at providing a quick fix. Often these are designed to ensure that the safety-net does not miss any at-risk children. These are naïve responses that do little to address the problem. Indeed, writers have argued that such solutions have the potential to increase the risk of child abuse for many children by destabilising families and creating an overburdened system that struggles to respond to children who really are at high risk (Scott, 2006).

The way forward is not about adopting reactive responses to child homicide. It is about understanding risk factors for children and understanding the ways in which family adversity accumulates. It is about understanding how to break cycles of abuse and neglect and strategically building the sector so it works as a coherent system for children.

Taking a life-course perspective

In Chapter 2 we introduced a typology for understanding accumulated family adversity, and the way in which factors associated with increased risk can accumulate from childhood and be reinforced across the life course. The potential for the typology is not its predictive value – indeed, it is likely that most people with one or many of the factors will never harm a child. Rather, its greatest strength rests in its capacity to inform a framework for understanding family need across the life cycle, and a blueprint for building the sector strategically to respond to that need.

Influenced by the family adversity typology, we will now expand the analysis to include risk factors associated with neglect and family violence, building a conceptual framework designed to understand vulnerabilities that accumulate across the life course contributing

Figure 7.2: A life-course framework for understanding vulnerability and resilience

Childhood vulnerabilities	Adolescent vulnerabilities	Adulthood vulnerabilities	Family resilience and protective factors
Harsh family discipline and parental strife	Poor/needy peer engagement	Entering abusive relationships	Adequate housing
Growing up in poverty	Low academic achievement	Multiple relationships	Meaningful employment, independence and self-reliance
Family violence victimisation	Prematurely independent	Poor conflict-resolution skills	Connectedness to family, cultural and community supports
State care with multiple caregivers	Early pregnancy	Inconsistent parenting	
	Truancy		
Sexual abuse	Sexual victimisation	Poor mental health, depression etc.	Connectedness to education and health providers
Submissive/ aggressive role development	Fringe criminality and/or aggressive offending before age 15	Drug and alcohol abuse	Changes in family belief systems and tolerance of violence
Disassociation		Suicide ideation	
Mental model of violence normalisation	Poor empathy development and impulse control	Emotional relationship/ bonding issues	Effective role models and mentors
Anxiety and hyper-vigilance	Drug and alcohol abuse	Regularly unemployed	Timely access to quality interventions
Poor attachment	Mental health issues (anorexia, obsessive and conduct disorders)	History of offending	Good assessment and treatment of parental issues
Boundary issues (role confusion, authority issues, risk-taking)	Poor parenting role modelling	Perpetrating family violence and child abuse	
Stigmatisation	Unemployment	Early parenthood	
Poor developmental milestones		Social isolation	
Poor life-modelling		Poor access to resources	

Reduction of risk and building individual and family resilience

← ← ← ← ←

to abusive and/or neglectful parenthood, and the resilience factors which can mitigate future risk (see Figure 7.2).

This life-course framework provides an understanding of the ways in which individual adversity can accumulate over time and increase risk for the next generation of children. It reinforces the need to focus on the underlying contributory factors associated with the parents, and on early responses to vulnerabilities that young children are developing, which can be addressed by accessing services from universal, targeted, and specialist systems, as shown in Figure 7.3.

Strategically building services that focus on critical developments during the life course requires more than just providing support services for struggling parents. It requires services that can respond to the specific needs of children. It also requires services for adolescents who will become tomorrow's parents. It requires specialist services for young people and adults who need to address drug and alcohol problems, mental health issues, and family violence. It requires

Figure 7.3: The scope of services

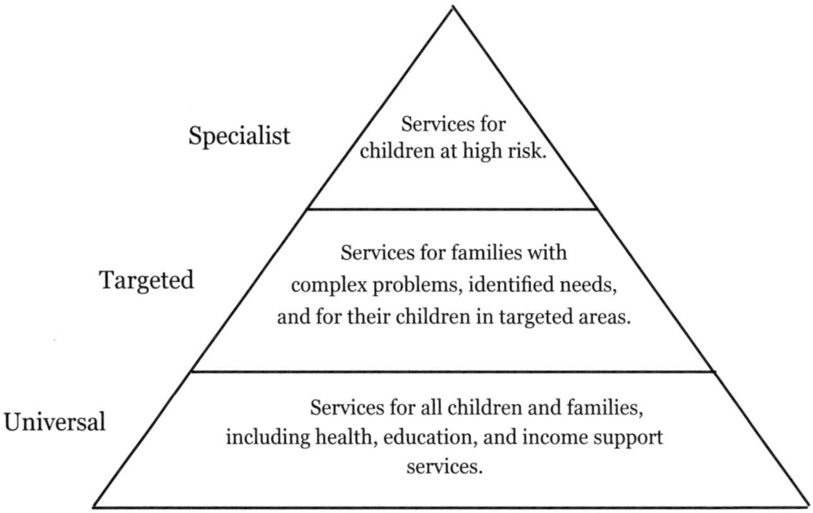

Specialist — Services for children at high risk.

Targeted — Services for families with complex problems, identified needs, and for their children in targeted areas.

Universal — Services for all children and families, including health, education, and income support services.

From: CYF & MSD (2006, p. 27). Reprinted with permission.

support services that young people and families choose to seek help from. Essentially it requires a public-health model of welfare involving universal, targeted, and specialist services.

Research clearly shows that intervening in a family-supportive way early in the life of a child brings the best long-term results. Early intervention helps children to do better socially and educationally, helps improve health and well-being, and can reduce violence within the family over the longer term. The strengthening and integration of different kinds of services (universal, targeted and specialist) is more likely to ensure that the right services are provided at the optimum time in the life of a family.

Building the sector strategically shifts us from ad hoc development toward a more coherent approach that prioritises services delivered by universal, targeted and specialist systems that build individual and family resilience. Using a 'family-need' framework to guide sector development will not only help to identify needs during critical periods of the life course (childhood, adolescence and parenthood), but also highlight where gaps exist and services need to be developed.

Any move toward a more focused public-health model of welfare would also need to take into account the diverse cultural mix of families in Aotearoa New Zealand. New Zealand's child welfare system is unique and the most successful future developments are likely to be those built around the strengths of our cultural systems. In the field of child welfare internationally this country is looked on as being innovative, largely because of its family-responsive law and the development of the Family Group Conference concept. In particular, its potential strength lies in legislative provisions that pave the way for iwi (and other cultural group) partnerships in child welfare and child care and protection service development. One of the challenges is to strengthen iwi (and other cultural) human services organisations that can, with agency support, meet the needs of their own families and children, something that was clearly envisaged in the Children, Young Persons and Their Families Act in 1989 when it originally passed into law.

Strong and vibrant services for Māori families that have developed over time in New Zealand provide a template for the kind of services that will enhance Māori health and well-being. Contemporary thinking around Māori wellness and health centre upon the theme of interconnectedness, generally described as 'holistic' (Durie, 1998, p. 72). Health is viewed as an inter-related phenomenon, integrative and harmonious with the environment. The whare tapa wha model of Māori health and well-being helps to illuminate four critical areas of well-being: taha wairua (spiritual dimension), taha hinengaro (emotional or mental dimension), taha tinana (physical dimension), and taha whānau (extended family dimension) (Durie, 1998). Existing agencies across the country provide services based on values that are fundamental to Māori kaupapa[22], and ongoing effort is needed to build on these initiatives and provide the support they need to carry out this important work.

New Zealand's child welfare system will risk lacking relevance for Māori if it fails to incorporate their views, values and perspectives. Building systems of response that resonate with cultural practices is more likely to impact positively and be accessed readily by Māori and Pacific families. Indeed, Durie (2003, p. 304) suggests, 'unless Māori had a sense of ownership any state programmes or policies would run the risk of being dismissed as modern versions of colonial prescriptions'. Culturally based human services will be essential to the development of appropriately responsive services, and any public-health model of welfare initiative will need to be developed in the context of culturally responsive service delivery.

In the end, building effective systems of welfare requires a complex mix of services that are purposeful in their response to the life-course needs of children and families. In recent years New Zealand has made significant advances toward the strengthening of early intervention services, forming the foundation of a sound public-health model. Child homicide, child abuse and neglect do not exist in isolation. They are correlated with 'low birth weight, child behavioural problems, low literacy levels of children, non-completion of school, juvenile crime, drug use, (and) teenage pregnancy' (Scott, 2006, p. 12). A system that recognises this complexity will not respond with quick fixes that do not endure. Effective systems will be those that provide lasting services and interventions across the life course, by understanding the unique needs of families and children at risk and by strategically crafting culturally responsive services that will protect and support children and families over time.

Notes

[19] D. Kane, Inspector General, Illinois Department of Children and Family Services, personal communication, May 15, 2006.

[20] D. Tipene Leach, personal communication, October 2006.

[21] Ferguson's use of 'conveyor belt' refers to a culture of practice that is focused on achieving targets and getting cases through the system, a practice that is considered to be at the expense of in-depth social work with families.

[22] See for example, He Waka Tapu, a Māori health and social service organisation that operates in the South island. He Waka Tapu provides services to prevent family violence, and to promote strong, healthy families that will foster intergenerational strength.

References

Armytage, P. & Reeves, C. (1992). Practice insights as revealed by child death inquiries in Victoria and overseas. In G. Calvert, A. Ford & P. Parkinson (Eds.), *The practice of child protection*. Sydney, NSW, Australia: Hale & Iremonger.

Barter, K. (2001). Building community: A conceptual framework for child protection. *Child Abuse Review*, 10(4) 262 –278.

Bell, L. (1999). A comparison of multi-disciplinary groups in the UK and New Jersey. *Child Abuse Review*, 8(5), 314–324.

Belsky, J. (1980). Child Maltreatment: An ecological integration. *American Psychologist*, 35, 320-35.

Berridge, D. & Cleaver, H. (1987). *Foster home breakdown*. Oxford: Blackwell.

Birmingham, J., Berry, M. & Bussey, M. (1996). Certification for child welfare protective services staff members: The Texas initiative. *Child Welfare*, 75(6), 727–740.

Briar-Lawson, K., Schmid, D. & Harris, N. (1997). The partnership journey: First decade. *Public Welfare*, 55(2), 4.

Brookman, F. & Nolan, J. (2006). The dark figure of infanticide in England and Wales: Complexities of diagnosis. *Journal of Interpersonal Violence*, 21(7), 869–889.

Burgess, R. & Youngblade, L. (1988). Social incompetence and the intergenerational transmission of abusive parental practices. In G. Hotaling, D. Finkelhor, J. Kirkpatrick & M Straus (Eds.), *Family abuse and its consequences: New direction in research*. London: Sage.

Busch, R. & Robertson, J. (1994). I didn't know just how far you could fight: Contextualising the Bristol Inquiry. Waikato Law Review, 2, 41–68.

Caspi, A., McClay, J., Moffitt, T.E., Mill, J., Martin, J., Craig, I.W., Taylor, A. & Poulton, R. (2002). Role of genotype in the cycle of violence in maltreated children. *Science*, 297, 851–854.

Cavanagh, K., Emerson Dobash, R. & Dobash, R. (2005). Men who murder children inside and outside the family. *British Journal of Social Work*, 35, 667–688.

Cheyne, C., O'Brien, M. & Belgrave, M. (1997). *Social policy in Aotearoa New Zealand: A critical introduction*. New York: Oxford University Press.

Child, Youth and Family & Ministry of Social Development. (2006). *Children at increased risk of death from maltreatment and strategies for prevention*. Wellington, NZ: Ministry of Social Development.

Connolly, M. (2004). *Child protection and family welfare: Statutory responses to children at risk*. Christchurch, NZ: Te Awatea Press.

Connolly, M. (2006). Practice frameworks: Conceptual maps to guide interventions in child welfare. *British Journal of Social Work*. Advance Access doi:10.1093/bjsw/bc.1049.

Connolly, M., Crichton-Hill, Y. & Ward, T. (2006). *Culture and child protection: Reflexive responses*. London: Jessica Kingsley.

Crow, G. & Marsh, P. (1997). *Family group conferences, partnership and child welfare: A research report on four pilot projects in England and Wales*. Sheffield, UK: University of Sheffield.

Department of Health. (1995). *Child Protection: Messages from research*. London: HMSO.

Department of Health and Social Security [DHSS]. (1985). *Social work decisions in child care*. London: HMSO.

Dingwell, R. (1989). Labelling children as abused or neglected. In W. Stainton Rogers, D. Hevey & E. Ash (Eds.), *Child abuse and neglect*. London: Batsford.

Doolan, M. (2006). Child homicide in New Zealand: 2001–2005. *Te Awatea Review*, 4, 25.

D'Orban, P. (1979). Women who kill their children. *British Journal of Psychiatry*, 134, 560–71.

Durie, M. (1998). *Whaiora: Māori health development* (2nd ed.). Auckland, NZ: Oxford University Press.

Durie, M. (2003). *Nga Hahui Pou: Launching Māori futures*. Wellington: Huia Publishers.

Fanslow, J., Chalmers, D. & Langley, J. (1995). Homicide in New Zealand: An increasing public health problem. *Australian Journal of Public Health*, 19, 50–57.

Ferguson, H. (2004). *Protecting children in time: Child abuse, child protection and the consequences of modernity*. Basingstoke, UK: Palgrave Macmillan.

Fergusson, D. M., Boden, J. M. & Horwood, L. J. (2006). Examining the intergenerational transmission of violence in a New Zealand birth cohort. *Child Abuse & Neglect*, 30(2), 89–108.

Goddard, C. (1998). Social workers' responses to repeated hostility in child abuse cases: The traditional social worker–client relationship or a new approach to hostage theory? In M. Slattery (Ed.), *Proceedings of the first national conference on child abuse: Facing the Future*. Melbourne, Australia: Victorian Society for the Prevention of Child Abuse and Neglect.

Hallett C. & Birchall, E. (1992). *Coordination and child protection: A review of the literature*. Edinburgh: HMSO.

Hansen, D., Conaway, L. & Christopher, J. (1990). Victims of child physical abuse. In R. Ammerman & M. Hersen (Eds.), *Treatment of family violence: A source book* (pp. 17–49). New York: Wiley.

Hassall, I. (2006). What is to be done about child homicide in New Zealand? Action for Children and Youth Aotearoa Inc., retrieved on 7 February 2007 from www.acya.org.nz/?t=62.

Herman-Giddens, M. (Ed.) (2001). *Not invisible, not in vain*. Raleigh, NC: North Carolina Child Advocacy Institute.

Hough, G. (1996). Using ethnographic methods to research the work world of social workers in child protection. In J. Fook (Ed.), *The reflective researcher: Social workers' theories of practice research*. St Leonards, NSW, Australia: Allen and Unwin.

Howitt, D. (1992). *Child abuse errors: When good intentions go wrong*. New York: Harvester Wheatsheaf.

Kelly, J. (1990). Treating the child abuser. In R. Ammerman & M. Hersen (Eds.), *Children at risk: An evaluation of factors contributing to child abuse and neglect*. New York: Plenum Press.

Kinley, L. & Doolan, M. (1997). *Patterns and reflections: Mehemea.* Wellington, NZ: Children, Young Persons and Their Families Service.

Kotch, J., Chalmers, D., Fanslow, J., Marshall, S. & Langley, J. (1993). Morbidity and death due to child abuse in New Zealand. *Child Abuse and Neglect*, 17, 233–247.

Krug, E., Dahlberg, L., Mercy, J., Zwi, A. & Lozano, R. (2002). *World report on violence and health.* Geneva, Switzerland: World Health Organization.

Lawrence, R. (2004). Understanding fatal assault of children: A typology and explanatory theory. *Children and Youth Services Review*, 26, 837–852.

Lawrence, R. & Irvine, P. (2004). Redefining fatal child neglect. *Child Abuse Prevention Issues*, 21. Melbourne, VIC, Australia: Australian Institute of Family Studies.

Liamputtong, P. & Ezzy, D. (2005). *Qualitative research methods* (2nd ed.). Melbourne, VIC, Australia: Oxford University Press.

Lupton, C. & Stevens, M. (1997). *Family outcomes: Following through on family group conferences* (SSRIU report No. 34). Portsmouth, UK: University of Portsmouth, Social Services and Information Unit.

MacDonald, G. (2002). Child Protection. In D. McNeish, T. Newman & H. Roberts (Eds.), *What works for children*. Buckingham, UK: Open University Press.

Mansell, J. (2006). The underlying instability in statutory child protection: Understanding the system dynamics driving risk assurance levels. *Social Policy Journal of New Zealand*, 28, 97–132.

McIntosh, J. (2000). Where service paths cross: Potential for innovative practice. *Proceedings of the Children, young people and domestic violence national forum: The way forward* (pp. 87–88). Barton, ACT, Australia: Office of the Status of Women.

McKeown, K. (2000). *Supporting families: A guide to what works in family support services for vulnerable families.* Dublin, Ireland: Department of Health and Children.

Munro, E. (2002). *Effective child protection.* London: Sage.

Munro, E. (2005). Improving practice: Child protection as a systems problem. *Children and Youth Services Review*, 27, 375–391.

Ministry of Social Development. (2002). *New Zealand living standards 2000.* Wellington, NZ: Ministry of Social Development.

Ministry of Social Development. (2004). *New Zealand families today.* Wellington, NZ: Ministry of Social Development.

Ministry of Social Development. (2007). The Social Report 2007. Wellington, NZ: Ministry of Social Development.

National Clearinghouse on Child Abuse and Neglect Information [NCCAN]. (2004). *Child abuse and neglect fatalities: Statistics and interventions.* Washington DC: NCCAN.

Newberger, E. & Bourne, R. (1985). *Unhappy families: Clinical and research perspectives on family violence.* Littleton, MA: Publishing Sciences Group.

Office of the Commissioner for Children [OCC]. (2000). *Final report on the investigation into the death of James Whakaruru.* Wellington, NZ: OCC.

Packman, J., Randall, J. & Jacques, N. (1986). *Who needs care?* Oxford: Blackwell.

Pecora, P., Whittaker, J. & Maluccio, A. (1992). *The child welfare challenge: Policy, practice and research.* New York: Walter de Gruyter.

Power, M. (1997). *The audit society.* Oxford: Oxford University Press.

Pritchard, R. (2001). A study of filicide in the context of dispute between parents: An investigation into indicators of risk. Unpublished manuscript, Victoria University of Wellington, School of Psychology.

Pryor, J. & Rodgers, B. (2001). *Children in changing families: Life after parental separation.* Oxford: Blackwell.

Reder, P., Duncan, S. & Gray, M. (1993). *Beyond blame: Child abuse tragedies revisited.* London: Routledge.

Ridley, M. (2003). *Nature via nurture: Genes, experience and what makes us human.* London: Fourth Estate.

Ridley, K. & Scott, S. (1999). Maximising the benefits of hindsight: A new model for intra-agency reviews of social work practice. *Social Work Now,* 14, 60–67.

Sankey, M. (2003). *Fatal assault and neglect of children and young people, NSW Child Death Review Team.* Sydney, NSW, Australia: Commission for Children and Young People.

Schlosser, P., Pierpont, J. & Poertner, J. (1992). Active surveillance of child abuse fatalities. *Child Abuse and Neglect*, 16, 3–10.

Scott, D. (2006, February). Sowing the seeds of innovation in child protection. Paper presented at the Tenth Australasian Conference on Child Abuse and Neglect, Wellington, NZ.

Spinetta, J. & Rigler, D. (1972). The child-abusing parent: A psychological review. *Psychological Bulletin*, 77, 296–304.

Stoesz, D. (2002). From social work to human services. *Journal of Sociology & Social Welfare*, 29(4), 19–38.

Stokstad, E. (2002). Violent effects of abuse tied to gene. *Science*, 297, p. 752.

Strang, H. (1996). *Children as victims of homicide. Trends and Issues.* Canberra, ACT, Australia: Australian Institute of Criminology.

Stroud, J. (2000). European child homicide studies: Quantitative studies and a preliminary report on a complementary qualitative research approach. *Social Work in Europe*, 7(3), 31–37.

Tomison, A. (2000). Exploring family violence. *Issues in child abuse prevention*, 13. Melbourne, VIC, Australia: Australian Institute of Family Studies.

Triseliotis, J. (1989). Foster care outcomes: A review of key research findings. *Adoption and Fostering*, 13, 5–17.

UNICEF (2003). *A league table of child maltreatment deaths in rich nations* (Innocenti Report Card No. 5). Florence, Italy: UNICEF Innocenti Research Centre.

Vondra, J. (1990). Sociological and ecological factors. In R. Ammerman & M. Hersen (Eds.), *Children at risk: An evaluation of factors contributing to child abuse and neglect*. New York: Plenum Press.

Walters, D. (1975). *Physical and sexual abuse of children: Causes and treatment*. Bloomington, IN: Indiana University Press.

Wilczynski, A. (1997). *Child homicide*. London: Greenwich Medical Media.

Wilson, S. (1997). Understanding child abuse tragedies. *Social Work Now*, 6, 23–29.

Worrall, J. (2001). Kinship care of the abused child: The New Zealand experience. *Child Welfare*, 80(5), 497–511.

Index

The Authors

Dr Marie Connolly holds the position of Chief Social Worker within the New Zealand Government. Previously she was Associate Professor and Director of the Te Awatea Violence Research Centre at the University of Canterbury. Widely published, she has written several books in her area of scholarship, her most recent being *Morals, rights and practice* with Tony Ward. Her research interests include child and family welfare and she has a social work background in statutory child welfare.

Mike Doolan, MSW (Distinction), is Adjunct Senior Fellow at the School of Social Work and Human Services at the University of Canterbury and was formerly Chief Social Worker within the New Zealand Government. He has an extensive practice background in child protection, child welfare and work with young people who offend. He has co-authored a book on kinship care and published in the fields of: family group conferences; violence in society; child homicide; and youth justice. He was made an Officer of the New Zealand Order of Merit in 2001.